NEW·LIBRARY·OF

PASTORAL·CARE

LETTING GO

Caring for the Dying and the Bereaved

Ian Ainsworth-Smith
and Peter Speck

First published 1982
SPCK
Holy Trinity Church
Marylebone Road
London NW1 4DU

Eleventh impression 1994

ISBN 0 281 03861 9

Filmset by Pioneer
Printed in Great Britain by
The Longdunn Press Ltd, Bristol

*To all those people, living and departed,
who have assisted our understanding in
many different ways*

Contents

List of Tables   viii

Foreword   ix

Introduction   xi

Acknowledgements   xii

1. Opportunity for Growth — Facing the Death of Another   1

2. Opportunity for Growth — Facing our own Death   15

3. Letting Go   34

4. The Context of Dying   44

5. Rites and Customs   61

6. When Grief Goes Wrong   106

7. The Minister Himself   114

Appendix A: Practicalities   130

Appendix B: Useful Addresses   137

Appendix C: Some Other Cultural Patterns   145

Select Bibliography   150

Index   152

List of Tables

'Normal' Patterns of Bereavement Behaviour   13

'Cones of Awareness': How the Dying
Person's View of the World may Change   32

'Grief Work' Illustration   57

Ways in which Family and Friends Helped the
Bereaved after the Death   87

What to Do when Someone Dies   133

Foreword

The *New Library of Pastoral Care* has been planned to meet the needs of those people concerned with pastoral care, whether clergy or lay, who seek to improve their knowledge and skills in this field. Equally, it is hoped that it may prove useful to those secular helpers who may wish to understand the role of the pastor.

Pastoral care in every age has drawn from contemporary secular knowledge to inform its understanding of man and his various needs and of the ways in which these needs might be met. Today it is perhaps the secular helping professions of social work, counselling and psychotherapy, and community development which have particular contributions to make to the pastor in his work. Such knowledge does not stand still, and pastors would have a struggle to keep up with the endless tide of new developments which pour out from these and other disciplines, and to sort out which ideas and practices might be relevant to his particular pastoral needs. Among present-day ideas, for instance, of particular value might be an understanding of the social context of the pastoral task, the dynamics of the helping relationship, the attitudes and skills as well as factual knowledge which might make for effective pastoral intervention, and perhaps most significant of all, the study of particular cases, whether through verbatim reports of interviews or general case presentation. The discovery of ways of learning from what one is doing is becoming increasingly important.

There is always a danger that a pastor who drinks deeply at the well of a secular discipline may lose his grasp of his own pastoral identity and become 'just another' social worker or counsellor. It in no way detracts from the value of these professions to assert that the role and task of the pastor are quite unique among the helping professions and deserve to be

clarified and strengthened rather than weakened. The theological commitment of the pastor and the appropriate use of
his role will be a recurrent theme of the series. At the same
time the pastor cannot afford to work in a vacuum. He needs
to be able to communicate and co-operate with those helpers
in other disciplines whose work may overlap, without loss of
his own unique role. This in turn will mean being able to
communicate with them through some understanding of their
concepts and language.

Finally, there is a rich variety of styles and approaches in
pastoral work within the various religious traditions. No
attempt will be made to secure a uniform approach. The
Library will contain the variety, and even perhaps occasional
eccentricity, which such a title suggests. Some books will be
more specifically theological and others more concerned with
particular areas of need or practice. It is hoped that all of
them will have a usefulness that will reach right across the
boundaries of religious denomination.

Introduction

The past few years have seen a proliferation in the number of books concerned with the dying and the bereaved. Most of these books deal with the psychological, medical and social aspects of dying and some have certainly become essential reading for those who care for the dying and their relatives. There is, however, not a great deal available on the more specific area of *pastoral* care for the dying and the bereaved.

This book is intended as a practical text for ministers of religion and for students in training. The authors have drawn upon their own experience and the insights gained from more extensive psychological studies, and have applied these to a demanding and fulfilling part of their ministry. The pastoral care of the dying and the bereaved is linked for many clergy with the name of Canon Norman Autton. In preparing this volume for the New Library of Pastoral Care we have been conscious of the contribution he has made to this aspect of caring.

The book has grown out of our experience, and we have been led to the belief that *grief* is the appropriate term to use when describing the reactions seen in both the dying and the bereaved. The dying person is grieving for the impending loss of his own life and the letting go of those whom he or she may love. The bereaved person's grief is a reaction to the anticipated or the actual loss of someone in close relationship. For this reason we have produced one book instead of two, with the unifying title of *Letting Go*.

The authors are both priests of the Church of England, but since we believe the text to be equally relevant and applicable to ministers of other traditions we have used the term 'minister' throughout. Our use of the masculine gender does not imply any desire to limit this area of ministry, since our experience has shown us what an important contribution female colleagues make. Whilst this book is primarily written for ministers of religion it is hoped that it will also be of value to other members of the caring professions, both in their own work and in promoting a better understanding of the positive contribution that clergy can make as partners in caring.

January 1982   IAN AINSWORTH-SMITH
PETER SPECK

ACKNOWLEDGEMENTS

We are indebted to the understanding and support of our respective wives and families during the writing of this book and for their own 'letting go' so that this work might come into being! Various other people have assisted us during the researching of material and have also given valuable criticism and advice as the manuscript grew: The staff of the Medical Libraries at the Royal Free Hospital and St George's Hospital, London: Deaconess Gwyneth Evans; The Revd Spencer V. Wilking; The Revd John Perryman; Rabbi Norman Solomon and other professional colleagues, patients and families in our respective hospitals and communities.

Our various notes, marginal jottings and amendments were brought together and retyped by Jean Ainsworth-Smith, to whom we express our sincere thanks.

Acknowledgement is also due to the following for permission to quote from published sources:

D. Reidel Publishing Company, for extracts from 'A Time to Live, A Time to Grieve' by Janice Reid, first published in *Culture, Medicine and Psychiatry* 3 (1979).

The National Society for Cancer Relief, for the list of facilities for cancer patients (Appendix B).

The Consumer Association, for the table from *What to do when Someone Dies*.

Her Majesty's Stationery Office, for the table 'Ways in which Family and Friends Helped the Bereaved after the Death', from *Families, Funerals and Finances* by P.J. Hennessy (1980).

ONE

Opportunity for Growth—Facing the Death of Another

*He that conceals his grief finds
no remedy for it.* (TURKISH PROVERB)

The death of someone you know and love can be a devastating
experience in which a large part of your world is lost. The
process by which we seek to fill the gap in our lives and to
find a new equilibrium is described as grief.

Sorrow is an essential ingredient of grief with an associated
pining for the world that has been lost, rather than for the
object itself. It is as if an important 'point of reference' has
disappeared in our lives and we are adrift until we can
establish new landmarks. To describe grief as a process
rightly implies that we are thinking of something occurring
over a period of time, and that its nature will change with
time.

Grief seems to run a more or less constant course but its
expression may be modified by various factors. The abrupt-
ness of the loss and the opportunity given to us to prepare for
the loss are important. The nature of the relationship between
the bereaved and the deceased as well as the previous
personality of the bereaved are also significant factors. Clearly
the death of a much loved husband will evoke a different
response from that consequent upon the death of a distant
uncle whom you never really liked. The ambivalence that
exists in many of our relationships can greatly influence our
reactions in the presence of death.

Sometimes the grief experience will enable us to use the
time to grow closer to those who are around us, but for some
it has the opposite effect in that it isolates and seems to push
us away from other people. In a similar way people may
either grow closer to God or alienate themselves from him

when they are faced with such a crisis. A person will
sometimes say, 'I just cannot believe in a God who lets such
things happen. My faith has been shattered.' The opportunity
for growth is there, but we may not always be able to grasp it.
The role of those who are around the dying and the bereaved
would seem to be that of giving the other person the *full right*
to feel and express his or her own feelings and thus enable
growth to take place. 'He that conceals his grief finds no
remedy for it.' If we are to enable people to work through
their grief then we need to understand and recognize some of
the reactions that may be experienced as we face the reality of
death and bereavement.

Craig Jenkins was six years of age when he had his
accident. His twelve-year-old brother (Wayne) had recently
had a new bike and Craig had pestered him constantly to
let him ride it, although it was too big for him. Because of
the way Craig always seemed to mess up his brother's
things Wayne had said no. One day after school, before his
brother arrived home, Craig took the bike out of the shed
and set off down the road, without telling his mother. At
the corner he failed to stop and went straight into the path
of a passing van. Craig sustained severe head injuries and
was rushed to hospital. The bike was ruined.

A neighbour ran to tell Craig's family what had happened
and Mrs Jenkins went to the hospital where her husband
later joined her.

At the hospital Craig was admitted to the Neurosurgery
Unit and his parents 'moved in'. The nursing staff, whilst
acknowledging their distress, found Craig's parents quite
difficult to support. They surrounded Craig with toys and
brought in a portable television and cassette recorder to
stimulate him into some response, in spite of being told
that he was deeply unconscious. Whenever staff requested
peace and quiet, or that the parents should have a break
and go for a walk, a meal, or some rest, they became very
aggressive and accused staff of trying to get rid of them,
but 'they knew their rights'. Meanwhile the sixteen-year-
old daughter, who had just started work, was left to look
after the house and the twelve-year-old brother.

The local vicar heard of the accident and visited the

hospital to see what was happening. Craig's mother looked apprehensive to see the vicar, but before he could say very much Craig's father told him to clear off. 'There's nothing you can say to me. What sort of God could stand back and let a kid suffer like this. You'd better go before I say or do something I shouldn't.' The vicar said that he would leave, but that he would keep in touch, that he understood Mr Jenkins's anger and if they wished would be willing to talk to them later when they calmed down. He added that they would pray for Craig in church. As the vicar left the ward, Mrs Jenkins followed him and said, 'I've only got a minute or I'll be in trouble, but thanks for coming. It gave me a shock to see you at first. I thought the staff had called you and that Craig was dying, but I know he will be all right. Craig always says his prayers at night, say one for him please.' With that she turned round quickly and went off in search of a toilet, where she could cry alone.

Craig's condition remained critical for several days and the parents stayed at the hospital only leaving the bedside alternately so that someone was always with him in case he woke up.

On the fourth day the staff suggested that the parents go together to the canteen for some food or a break. Mrs Jenkins thought that a good idea and eventually her husband agreed provided the cassette recorder was left on while they were away. Twenty minutes after they had left the ward Craig died. The parents were very distressed and Mr Jenkins became very abusive and aggressive towards the staff-nurse who had suggested they leave the ward. His wife meanwhile was oblivious to this and sat holding Craig and talking to him as if he were still alive. She seemed completely dazed and unable to take in that he had died. Then she began to cry and sat in the chair rocking to and fro saying, 'Why, why, why?' One of the nursing staff stood next to her with her arm around Mrs Jenkins. Mr Jenkins, having vented his wrath, came across to his wife. He touched his son on the head, then kissed his forehead and, turning to his wife, said, 'He's gone to sleep. Say goodnight and come home.' When they reached home and started to explain to their family what had happened the reality of the death began to sink in.

The vicar was contacted about the funeral. When he visited the family he found that the front room of the house had been cleared of all furniture and that Craig's coffin was in the centre of the room surrounded by toys. Mr Jenkins was clearly very ambivalent about the vicar (as was the vicar about Mr Jenkins!) but Mrs Jenkins seemed to see him as an ally who understood how she felt. Wayne (the twelve-year-old brother) was very withdrawn and would not go into the front room or talk to anyone about Craig. He stayed upstairs most of the time, watching television. It was assumed that he would not attend the funeral, but on the day he came downstairs dressed ready to go and silently got into the car. A lot of people attended the funeral and there were masses of flowers. After the funeral Mrs Jenkins talked of 'having lost her baby', and several people advised her to 'get pregnant, it's the best thing'. Craig's part of the bedroom was kept as if he were expected home — a shrine. His brother, who shared the bedroom, became very disturbed and got into trouble for shoplifting and vandalism. Mr Jenkins seemed to get very angry with his wife and to drink quite a bit. On one occasion he blamed her for not supervising Craig properly or checking that he could not get hold of the bike. When Mrs Jenkins became pregnant she was determined it should be a boy and that they should call him Craig. Gradually the parents were becoming estranged. Mrs Jenkins started going to church and prayed constantly that her baby would be a 'new Craig'. She felt that her husband did not understand her as well as the vicar did. The vicar was very concerned about Mrs Jenkins's attitude to the expected new baby and expressed his concern to the G.P. whom he knew very well, so that he could keep it in mind at her next ante-natal appointment, and suggested that they worked towards a joint meeting between the G.P./vicar/and the Jenkins family. Eventually this meeting took place.

It was a highly emotionally charged meeting and, whilst it was clear that Mrs Jenkins had persuaded her husband to attend, the couple were able to share some of their feelings about Craig's death and the new baby.

It was only a beginning, but hopefully it would be the commencement of a growing together and that, instead of

Craig's death pushing the family apart, they might begin to draw closer together.

Shock and Disbelief

Mr and Mrs Jenkins were clearly very shocked to hear of Craig's accident and found it hard to accept that he might not recover. They seem to say that if only they could have stimulated him sufficiently they would have proved the hospital wrong. The rest of the family almost ceased to exist as they focused all their attention on Craig, with the result that their world shrank to the size of the bed-space which he occupied. Although things were happening around them and people were explaining things to them, none of it seemed to be real or to 'connect'. Many people describe a sense of numbness—'It's almost like living in a big ball of cotton wool'.

The shock may also present itself in a physical way, coming in waves lasting from twenty minutes to about an hour: deep sighing, lack of strength and appetite, choking sensations and breathlessness, shivering and sometimes physical pain. Grief can sometimes be a very physical thing. C. S. Lewis writes:

> No one ever told me that grief felt so like fear. I am not afraid, but the sensation is like being afraid. The same fluttering in the stomach, the same restlessness, the yawning. I keep on swallowing.[1]

Talking about the impending death or the deceased tends to bring on these feelings and so the person may avoid situations and people who may trigger them off—including clergy on occasion. With Mr and Mrs Jenkins they seemed to be defending themselves from any talk of Craig dying by the use of the cassette recorder, television and their anger.

Denial of the death, or the likelihood of death, may take several forms and may last, usually, from a few hours to about two weeks. The form which the denial takes is influenced by our previous experiences of loss and separation, as well as by cultural factors. One may find a whole range from verbal denial, 'Oh, no! It isn't true' or 'I want a second opinion' (or hospital or miracle) to incapacitation (a stunned silence) or the performance of inappropriate actions (talking to the deceased and expecting a reply). Mrs Jenkins sat holding Craig and talking to him *after he died*, before she began to cry and ask, 'Why, why, why?'

Awareness

Gradually the shock and disbelief give way to a variety of different feelings which may flow back and forth like the tide, as awareness dawns.

Crying and feelings of physical emptiness are very common at this time, though not everyone will shed tears openly. Mrs Jenkins, for example, did not wish to cry in front of her husband, but waited until she could go to the toilet and be alone. Allowing someone to cry is different from implying that they ought to cry. We should beware of statements such as 'You'd feel a lot better if you had a good cry', which sound judgemental in that they imply we think the person is acting abnormally by not crying.

Pining. Once the death has occurred the relative may well pine for the deceased and search for them with an aimless wandering around the house, neighbourhood or hospital. Pining is often accompanied by a sense of emptiness. One lady, following a stillbirth, described herself as a Henry Moore statue with a large hollow space where her stomach should have been. Sometimes the bereaved will see or hear the deceased and they will either find this very comforting or frightening. This experience will either happen during the day or as a very vivid dream which causes upset when the person wakes up and realizes it was only a dream. One widow telephoned her vicar in a very distraught state to say that she thought she must be going mad. She had just prepared supper when she heard her husband (who had died two months before) put his key in the door-lock and come in. She then *saw* him hang his coat in the hall, enter the living room and sit in his favourite chair. When she fetched his supper from the kitchen he had disappeared. She screamed and dropped the meal. She needed a great deal of reassurance from her vicar that she was not going mad and that this experience was quite normal. Provided these reactions are not unduly prolonged they should not cause too much concern. However, if they become very prolonged or lead to the setting up of a shrine — as in the case of the bedroom in the Jenkins's household — then this can be an indication that people may not be progressing through their grief.

Anger is a very common part of grief for many people and there was plenty of it in evidence within the Jenkins family! This anger is frequently displaced in three directions: against medicine, against God, against the deceased or self.

Mr and Mrs Jenkins displayed quite a bit of anger towards the staff of the hospital at different times. Whilst they were grateful to the staff for what they were doing for Craig, nevertheless they were suspicious that the hospital might 'give up' too soon and so they became angry at any attempt to make them see reality or to leave the bedside. Because many relatives feel inadequate in the face of acute illness this can lead to angry criticism of the care given by the staff, as a way of showing that the relatives care.[2] Sometimes this anger is directed at the hospital doctor (for being unable to cure), at the general practitioner (for not diagnosing the condition earlier), or the ambulance service (for the delay in collecting the patient from home).

It is likely that Craig's parents experienced, but could not express and acknowledge, aggression towards Craig himself for behaving stupidly and causing so much pain to everyone. One young father, whose wife had just delivered a stillborn child, sat holding their dead baby. He was very angry with the child and in a loud voice said to the child, 'What right had you to die when we had planned for you, wanted you and had everything ready for you?' Anger against the person who has died is often repressed because others may not understand, or may not allow us to express it. Craig's brother seemed to have a lot of repressed anger, against his brother and his parents. This was not only because of the loss of his bike but also because *his* feelings were not being acknowledged by anyone. It was his sister who eventually helped him with these feelings because she too felt similarly about the way her new job was being spoilt. She was also instrumental later in reminding her parents of the need to replace the bike, but Wayne's negative feelings had already gone deep.

Many people feel that a faith in God provides a sort of Divine Assurance Policy against anything unpleasant happening. When things do go wrong in life we may, therefore, feel that God has let us down and so we become angry with him, but try not to show it. The entry of the vicar acted as a focus for much that Mr Jenkins was feeling.

The vicar's presence in the ward served to crystallize the seriousness of Craig's condition because Mr and Mrs Jenkins were reacting to the stereotyped image of the clergy as the 'associates of undertakers', or as 'vultures' who arrive shortly before the death and whose presence may, in some strange way, actually bring about the death. To another family the arrival of a minister would be welcomed because their stereotype image might be that of a friend and a source of comfort and strength. Care is needed before using words such as 'Go forth, thou Christian soul' unless one has found out where the family are in their grief. If they are still denying the reality of impending death then these words may create fear and antipathy and the rejection of the priest's ministry. Some people who have little experience of the Church's ministry may even feel that because of the minister's authority (and 'hot-line' to God), if he uses the words 'Go forth', then the soul will. Therefore, the longer the minister is kept away the longer they can continue their pretence. Sensitivity and awareness of people's understanding of what the minister is doing are very important.

The clergy also represent God and, as in the case of Mr Jenkins, people are sometimes very angry with God for 'allowing such things to happen'. Sometimes the clergy will receive verbal, and occasionally physical, assault in such situations because the person cannot get hold of God but can get hold of the minister! Mr Jenkins was fairly restrained and simply said, 'You'd better go before I say or do something I shouldn't'. Mrs Jenkins, perhaps without realizing what she was doing, tried to placate the vicar and God and to ask him to intercede for her son's life. The way in which we cope with these angry feelings and respond to them is very important, for if we do not handle them properly they can very easily hinder growth. We shall return to this topic later.

Guilt is frequently associated with anger and is often expressed in the 'if only' questions. There is often a strong feeling in the minds of many people that there must be someone to blame for the death that has occurred or is about to occur. Therefore guilt and blame are frequently mixed in with the anger voiced against various people. Sometimes this guilt is well founded in that somebody was negligent or did contribute towards the death. We might term this *real guilt.* Real guilt is the type that one sees most frequently, where the cause and effect are clearly recognizable: the motorist who reverses his car without due care and knocks over a child; the alcoholic whose self-abuse has led to chronic liver failure; or those moments when under stress we say something very hurtful to someone else and regret it later. The fact that cause and effect may be easily identifiable does not mean that these feelings will necessarily be readily accepted.

Irrational or exaggerated guilt arises when our experience of guilt is out of all proportion to the event said to be causing it: 'If only I had made my son finish his breakfast before dashing off to school he wouldn't have been on that street corner at the time the lorry ran out of control'; or 'If only we had not had a row a month ago my husband would not be dead now'; or 'If only I had recognized earlier that he was unwell and looked after him better'. This form of guilt can sometimes lead to self-punishment in order to atone and in some way restore things to how they were. The vast array of toys with which the Jenkins family surrounded their son in hospital, and his coffin at home, seemed to be both an expression of their wanting to care, but also a means of salving their consciences for what had happened. In a similar way people may give large sums of money to the Church or to charities as a means of easing feelings of guilt in their relationship with God. One of the key roles of the clergy in respect of the guilt feelings of the bereaved is to help them to grow in their understanding of the meaning of reconciliation, forgiveness and the identification of self-punishing behaviour. In the words of Tillich, this means to foster in the person 'the courage to accept oneself as accepted in spite of being unacceptable'.[3]

This brings us to the third type of guilt which might be described as *existential guilt.* This is a nebulous area related to deeply rooted feelings of inadequacy and the acceptance of our own mortality and weaknesses. In the face of death, whether our own or that of someone else, we tend to look back over our life and reflect on words, actions and relationships and to judge ourselves according to the extent of our sense of human failure and to make excuses for it. Following the exposure of some personal failure, or its realization, existential guilt may be expressed when we excuse ourselves by saying, 'It's just the way I'm made, I can't help it'. Some guilt, therefore, is related to existence itself, to the anxiety of self-rejection and to moral self-awareness and existential doubt[4] which is often displayed in the question, 'What have I done to deserve this?' In the case of Mrs Jenkins, after the initial shock had worn off, she simply sat holding Craig and saying, 'Why, why, why?' In that Mrs Jenkins was beyond words at this time it would not have helped for the vicar to have tried to answer her 'why' questions at this time. Coping with such existential feelings of guilt and doubt can be an important growing point in the grief process. The development of courage to face these questions and feelings can lead us to live life more fully and to become more at-one with our humanity and our own limitations.

Depression. Episodes of sadness and depression are very understandable and natural following the death of someone close to you. It is like having a heavy weight placed on you, so that every task takes longer to perform and even the simplest things become a burden. This is often accompanied by a sense of futility and feelings of isolation. 'What's the point, who is going to see, why should I bother?'[5] These episodes are usually only transient and within the space of the same day one can move from sadness to a more normal mood. In contrast the depressed person, as opposed to the grief-stricken person, will be more persistently downcast and pessimistic, will not usually respond to warmth and reassurance, and will have a lasting sense of inner emptiness. It is important to distinguish the depressive episodes of grief from the severe depression which requires appropriate referral for professional help.

Usually when the bereaved person is feeling depressed he or she will withdraw from people because they will feel themselves to be unlovable and a leper: 'I taint people with death and I make them feel uncomfortable'. Feelings of low self-esteem may lead to harsh self-judgements, and those seeking to help need to be warm in their approach and positive. It is important to help the person towards a more objective and accurate balance sheet of their life. Death also produces a feeling of helplessness and impotence in that we feel unable to influence what happens to us. This can lead us to echo the words of Alexander Pope, 'Past hope, past cure, past help'. Fortunately such feelings do not last long but the bereaved person does want the feeling to be accepted for what it is and not to be told to 'snap out of it' or 'pull yourself together'. Although such episodes may recur frequently, listening with acceptance and genuine warmth and understanding goes a long way towards lifting the oppressive feelings of depression from the grief stricken. Prolongation of such episodes usually indicates the need for professional help.

The various feelings that have been described with reference to the Jenkins family, and others, tend to flow back and forth during the process of grief. To continue the analogy used earlier, it is rather like the tide coming in and out each day. Each time the tide comes up the beach you don't know what it will leave behind as it recedes. One day anger, another time depression, another outbursts of grief. Although analogies can mislead, this way of describing the process at least helps us to appreciate that over the course of time we experience a variety of feelings, not in a set order and sometimes recurring. Some of the feelings, as we have seen with the Jenkins family, can be very strong and may lead people to think in terms of sedation. This may occasionally be necessary medically, but we should always ask whether the decision about sedation is to enable the bereaved to cope or to help us to cope. Usually one finds that the use of sedation leads to the postponement of grief and not its resolution. Sedation by alcohol has a similar effect also!

Resolution

Eventually, the various conflicts and feelings are resolved and a new identity begins to be established. This takes many months and one usually thinks in terms of at least eighteen months to two years before one expects to see any completion of mourning. The time-scale can be affected by many things.

If the person is able, and has time, to commence their grieving before the death occurs then this will affect the process in that some of the reactions will have been worked through before the death occurs. However, when the actual death happens it does not mean that these feelings will not re-occur, but usually they will not be so forceful.

On the other hand, drowning your sorrows, as Mr Jenkins tried to do, merely prolongs grief in that you are avoiding it temporarily but it still remains to be faced. Mrs Jenkins was also trying to find a way to avoid working through her grief in that her new baby had to be a new Craig so that she could put the clock back and almost pretend it hadn't happened. With the vicar, Mrs Jenkins was putting him in the role of the nice, kind, understanding 'husband' who understood her better than her own husband. She retreated into fantasy and, quite rightly, the vicar recognized the need for professional help.

The process of resolution has several aspects:

1. To resolve that one *will* cope with the loss though it is not always easy to think of oneself as 'widowed' or 'childless'.

2. The frequent idealizing of the deceased, which often occurs earlier on.

3. The sense of detachment which comes from this idealization and which brings the ability to think and discuss the deceased realistically and comfortably.

4. A final resolution that one can enjoy oneself again and make new social contacts, without feeling disloyal to the deceased. Cultural factors are important here, as are organizations such as Cruse in helping the bereaved to accept a new status in society.

The Table on p. 13 summarizes many of the reactions that we have discussed and offers a tentative time-scale for normal bereavement behaviour.

The funeral *can* be a very important part of the grief process in that it can provide an opportunity and atmosphere for the expression of feelings that we may feel unable to express elsewhere. Within the context of the funeral the bereaved is removed from some of the constraints that may prevent the expression of grief. In some cultures there are

'Normal' patterns of bereavement behaviour

	DENIAL	DEVELOPING AWARENESS	RESOLUTION
	Death of spouse up to 2 weeks	2 weeks - 2 years	2 years - 5 years
Physical reactions	Shock	Loss of vitality. Physical symptoms of stress. Irrational behaviour — often coming in waves lasting 20 - 60 mins. Psycho-somatic illness, often parallels symptoms of deceased. (May not be reversed.)	
Emotional	Numbness	Outbursts of grief (pining, crying, exhaustion)	"Resolution"
	Cottonwool feeling	Depression or Sadness	1. The resolve that one will cope
	Denial	Anger — against deceased, medicine, God ('why')	2. Sense of detachment allowing freedom of action
		Loss of confidence and self-approval	3. Feeling it is now O.K. to enjoy social contacts etc.
		Guilt ('if only . . .')	
		Loneliness — especially in older bereaved	
		Idealizing of the deceased	
External factors affecting behaviour	Circumstances of death and funeral arrangements	Financial loss or gain	Acceptance of new status by society. Role of organisations such as:- Cruse
	Family	Loss of status	
	Religious beliefs and culture	Anniversaries	Society for Compassionate Friends
		Society's disapproval of overt emotion and avoidance of death	

N.B. Grief work may commence prior to the death of the patient.

official mourners and 'wailers' whose role is to initiate the expression of deep emotion. We shall return to a discussion of the place of the funeral in the grief process later (see chapter 5).

The first anniversary can be especially painful for the bereaved as can events such as Christmas and birthdays, which can thrust the person back into earlier grief reactions for a short period. This can happen even if, to all intents and purposes, the person has resolved their grief. Similarly a subsequent death or major loss can have the effect of re-awakening the previous grief.

Grief is a very complex process and so it is not surprising, therefore, that for some it continues for a long time, or is never really completed, whilst for others it seems to progress gradually *without the need for any sort of intervention* except for a sensitive listening ear. If we are able to relate to the bereaved person and to be alongside them as a warm human being then perhaps we will be able to absorb the anger, together with the depressed and withdrawn periods. By accepting the other person with any ambivalent or negative feelings that they may have, we may thus be able to give the person the freedom to express grief in his or her own way, and so to use this experience of loss as an opportunity for growth.

Notes

1. C. S. Lewis, *A Grief Observed* (Faber, 1973), p. 7.
2. P. W. Speck, 'The Hospital Visitor', *Nursing Times* (5 July 1973).
3. P. Tillich, *The Courage to Be* (Fontana, 1979), p. 160.
4. ibid., p. 58.
5. C. S. Lewis, in *A Grief Observed*, describes this as the laziness of grief.

TWO

Opportunity for Growth—Facing our own Death

And how, if you were to die yourself? You know you must.
Only be ready for it by the preparation of a good life, and then
it is the greatest good that ever happened to thee.
(JEREMY TAYLOR, HOLY LIVING: HOLY DYING)

The prospect of personal death is an uncomfortable one for most people and is usually only contemplated when circumstances force us to do so. Our attitudes towards life, death and life after death will influence how we react to the realization that we may soon die. Equally important will be the manner in which death comes and our fear of pain, loss of dignity, and anxiety about those we leave behind. The extent to which we are able to cope with these anxieties will determine the extent to which we can agree with Jeremy Taylor in saying that death can be the 'greatest good that ever happened to thee'.

Colin and Anne were in their mid-thirties and had been married for fourteen years. They had two children, John aged thirteen years and Mary aged ten years. Colin had a good job with a firm of architects and they had recently moved into a new house with a larger mortgage commitment. Anne was a nurse and had recently gone back to nursing part-time. Colin had felt generally unwell for several weeks. Then he began to have a series of very heavy nosebleeds and over one weekend developed a great sense of weakness. By Monday he felt very ill and Anne called the doctor who referred Colin to the local hospital where the specialist admitted him to the ward for tests and blood transfusion.

Several days later, at the end of visiting time, Anne was

seen by one of the doctors. He told her that the initial tests had been completed and that they believed Colin to have leukaemia. He said that, as a nurse, she would appreciate what that meant, but they wished to give Colin more blood and to put him onto drug therapy in the hope that they might induce a remission. He suggested that at this early stage, since mental attitude was important, they should only tell Colin that he had severe anaemia. Somewhat numbed and shocked Anne nodded and left the office. She found her way to the hospital chapel and sat there, crying, for a long time until she felt calm enough to make her way home. Anne's parents lived nearby and because of their close relationship with Anne and Colin were a great support to Anne in the months that followed the diagnosis of Colin's illness.

Colin made a good response to treatment and, since he was feeling so much better, seemed to accept that it was anaemia which was now under control. He did not ask anyone what had caused the anaemia. He was discharged home, resumed work, and made periodic visits to the out-patient clinic. Over the months that followed Colin was admitted to hospital several times for blood transfusions, but usually only stayed overnight. Because Colin worked as an architect he was able to work at home on the days when he felt unable to travel to the office and the spare bedroom was fitted out as a 'drawing office'.

When the initial shock had worn off, Anne decided to keep the knowledge of the diagnosis to herself and her parents. She looked to her parents for support as she sought to readjust to what she now knew. She read about leukaemia and prayed that all would be well. Anne found it hard to keep the knowledge from her husband and felt very deceitful. However, she also felt it was not yet the right time to share it with Colin and managed, for the most part, to shut it from her mind. About eighteen months after diagnosis, Colin was taken ill again and readmitted into hospital. During the course of a ward round Colin over-heard a medical student use the word 'leukaemia'. He felt cold inside and found that he could not think straight. Later he tried to convince himself that the student had been talking about someone else, but the nagging doubt remained.

Colin became very withdrawn and would not say why. The following night he slept badly and at about 1 a.m. a young student nurse offered him some cocoa. He told her very curtly that it was not cocoa that he wanted and she asked why he had suddenly become so restless. He said, 'I know I'm going to die, I heard the doctors say so'. Not quite sure what to say the nurse said, 'I think you must have misunderstood and I will get night sister to come and talk to you'. When the night sister arrived Colin was quiet for a while and then told her what he had overheard. He said that, if it were true, then he wished to know all the facts about the illness and the treatment. The night sister then called the doctor who came and apologized for the way in which Colin had learnt his diagnosis and then Colin, the night sister and the doctor sat down and discussed the illness, treatment and the possibility of further remissions. At first Colin was very angry at the way in which he had been 'fooled' into believing it was anaemia, but he later admitted that he hadn't asked any questions about his illness because he was afraid to. The doctor let Colin express his anger with the hospital, with his wife and with himself for not questioning more. Colin thanked him for 'levelling with him' and then asked to be left alone.

The next morning Colin telephoned his wife and asked her to come to visit him as soon as the children had gone to school. When she arrived he told her what had happened the previous evening and then he cried for the first time. Later Colin became very practical and produced a lot of notes that he had written the night before, detailing what needed to be done about the mortgage, insurance policies, will and some of the jobs that he still had to finish for his firm. Although it was very stressful for them both they subsequently commented that they felt much more peaceful and calm after they had shared what each knew and feared. The conspiracy of silence was ended, Colin was now very tired and went off into a deep sleep.

Colin and Anne later asked for a second opinion and this was arranged. In fact Colin was seen by several consultants and the diagnosis of leukaemia was confirmed. His condition deteriorated over the next few weeks and he needed a great deal of reassurance from Anne that she and the family would cope if he died. He frequently said that he felt he had let her down in becoming ill and that he wished they could have longer. The children, who knew that Dad was seriously ill, became very helpful in and around the home—doing many of the things that he used to do to show that things were not falling apart without Dad. In some ways perhaps they coped too well, from Colin's point of view.

The hospital chaplain and Colin had formed a good relationship. During one of the chaplain's visits Colin expressed some of his anger and sense of unfairness that this should happen to him. 'I wish that I could see my children grow up and settle in life. I suppose you could not put in a good word upstairs, could you?' At times Colin would be very withdrawn and would not speak to anyone. At other times he would be writing off to travel agents for holiday brochures and making plans for a big family holiday. There were occasions when Colin would be very nasty with Anne (usually when the children were not visiting) and seemed to resent the fact that she was healthy. He would reduce her to tears and then be filled with remorse for the way he had behaved. On one such occasion Colin accused Anne of having an affair with someone else, said that she would be glad when he was dead so that she could have an active man again. After this latter outburst Anne left the ward hurriedly and went to the chapel in great distress where she was found by the chaplain. Gradually, after many tissues and some coffee, she explained what had happened and he was able to help her to see that Colin could only hit out at her. Because of their love for each other Colin felt it safe to vent his wrath on Anne. If he hit out at the nurses or doctors they might tell him 'to get on with it alone'. Then Anne and the chaplain talked about some of the fears and anxieties that Colin had. He was finding it almost intolerable to face 'letting go' of wife, family and life itself. He was afraid of dying (though not of death) and feared dying in pain or losing his dignity. The drugs he had received had already led to loss of his hair although it was now growing again. There had been times when Anne had found Colin withdrawn and she had felt rejected — especially when she found he was talking to the chaplain about certain feelings and reactions and not to her!

As a result of this discussion Anne was able to accept that Colin needed someone from outside the family to whom he could talk confidentially. The next day the chaplain visited while Anne and Colin were together. He asked Colin, 'How did you both meet?' Then as they talked about their first meeting he gradually led them to talk about their courtship, marriage, birth of the children. Bit by bit they were being put in touch once again with their earlier life together and, amidst much laughter, remembering many of the funny things that had happened to them. When they reached the time of Colin's illness Colin was quiet for a while and then said, 'We've had a very good life, haven't we?'

Colin and Anne were both communicant members of the Church of England and Colin asked about anointing and healing. Following discussion it was arranged that the chaplain should bring them both Communion later in the day and that they should be anointed. The chaplain spoke to their parish priest, who had kept in touch with Colin and Anne, and he arranged to come to the ward and take part in the service. The children and the ward sister also joined them for the service, after which Colin and Anne remarked on the sense of peace which they both felt. In the days that followed everyone seemed to be as prepared as they could be for Colin's death, whilst still enjoying the life that he had left.

Then Colin went into remission and the medical staff were talking about him 'going home'! The reactions in all concerned were a mixture of pleasure, joy, apprehension and disbelief. Two days after his discharge the chaplain received a telephone call from Colin. 'It's a weird feeling,' he said, 'I feel that I am having to be born into my own family all over again. It's as if I have come back from the dead.' It took quite a while for the family to readjust to being a 'Mum, Dad and two children' again, and Anne's parents and the local vicar were very important in helping them to settle down. The family had been facing up to the implications of Colin's diagnosis for so long that they had worked through a lot of their grief and so were almost waiting for his death—which had not happened. They were left with a strange feeling of guilt and resentment and pleasure that he was still with them. At the back of their minds was the anxiety that sooner or later they might have to face this all over again. A few months later there was another telephone call from Colin to say that things were one hundred per cent better and that, if anything, the whole experience had led Colin and Anne to fall in love all over again.

A year later Colin had to be readmitted to hospital where he failed to respond to treatment. Colin slept a great deal and did not say very much. Anne and her mother were sitting with him when he died, very peacefully and calmly. Although the family were thrown back into their grief there was a real feeling that they had grown during the previous two years and that Colin's death could not be described as a failure. They had learnt to 'let go' and to grow on. As Anne was later able to say, 'It sounds odd perhaps, but through Colin's illness and death I feel that we have all grown—including Colin!'

The reactions of Colin are similar to those experienced by many people when they realize that they must face the fact of personal death. His reactions also parallel those already described in relation to the bereaved following a death, the difference being that the dying person is grieving for the *impending loss* of his or her own life. The grief reaction of the family also frequently commences before the death occurs and thus provides another reason for the parallel reactions of Shock and Disbelief: Growing Awareness: Resolution.

Shock and Disbelief

The bereaved frequently experience shock following the death, and for the dying person the knowledge that one might soon die precipitates a crisis with accompanying feelings of shock, panic and an inability to believe it. This was certainly the case for Colin who tried to convince himself that the medical student was talking about someone else when he used the word 'leukaemia'. The extent to which we deny the knowledge is often related to our preparedness to receive the news and the way in which it is imparted to us.

A dying person receives communications from many people and on occasions these messages may be confused and ambiguous thus creating anxiety. Other communications may match the thoughts and feelings of the patient and help the person to make sense of what is being experienced. Some of the ways in which we receive information include:

1. Direct statements from doctor, nurse or other person.
2. Overheard comments made by staff, family or others.
3. Changes in treatment, position of bed in ward, etc.
4. Changes in behaviour observed in other people.
5. Self-diagnosis—reading medical dictionaries!
6. Alteration of symptoms, especially if they do not fit in with what you have already been told or led to expect.
7. An alteration in the attitude of others towards your future plans or job prospects.

The dying person will sometimes say, when the shock has worn off, that they knew deep down that 'things were not good'. Although they may have denied their diagnosis to themselves and to others the above sources of information have often conveyed the seriousness of their condition. This may be borne out by such comments as: 'It was their eyes that told me. They smiled with their mouths, but their eyes were sad'; or 'After the results came back the doctors didn't stay long with me, or would avoid me. I felt written off'. Colin requested all the information he could get about his condition, partly so that he knew what he had to face and partly so that he could confirm his worst fears. He was fortunate in having medical and nursing staff who would recognize his need and respond with an honest sharing of information. Sometimes our own anxieties about death and dying block any real sharing and lead instead to evasion and avoidance.

It is clear, therefore, that whatever *we* may decide about sharing what we know concerning the patient's prognosis the dying person will have already received a lot of communication from those around him and made various deductions of his own. Anyone who has gone through a range of tests, investigations, operation and subsequent treatment will have reached some conclusion, even if this has not been discussed with others. It is only as we build up a relationship of trust and confidence that the sick person will feel that perhaps it is safe to share some of their feelings and fears.

If such a relationship has been formed it is often more a matter of letting oneself be told than actually telling the other person what is happening to them. For the minister a question such as 'What has the doctor or hospital been able to tell you?' will be fairly open-ended. It allows the sick person to reveal what they know or suspect but also gives them the opportunity to terminate this line of approach with a brief 'Nothing much, you know what hospitals are'.

There should be no set rules about what people are, or are not, told. Getting close enough to the dying person is the only way to resolve this question because the sort of information we may be giving (or withholding) is best shared in a loving, caring relationship. There also needs to be lateral consultation with others who are providing care.

It is important not to tell lies to patients, but this does not imply telling the whole truth all at once. The prognosis or outlook may change, the understanding of the 'truth' may alter, and so one should gradually reveal more as you know it and the patient indicates that he wishes to receive it. Certainly, where the patient is asking 'How long have I got?' we should avoid rigid answers. It is often better to say 'months rather than years' than to give a rigid 'two months'. A rigid and definitive time can have the effect of extinguishing hope, and we should beware of removing hope.

The answer to the question 'To tell or not to tell' lies more in our preparedness to get close to those who are dying, finding out what *they* wish to know, and then having the courage to share the reality with them.

Because the dying, not surprisingly, find it hard to believe that they may not recover from their illness, they will frequently seek several 'other opinions' in the hope that another hospital, doctor or treatment centre may be able to offer a better prognosis or cure. Sometimes this will lead to visits to healing centres where the sick person or family may seek a miracle. So often physical healing may not occur but there may be a real healing of attitude and approach to the illness. Not all visits to healing centres are an expression of disbelief of a diagnosis, but this possibility should be borne in mind when discussing such centres with terminally ill people. Ministers may also need to remember that this may apply to the person's expectations of the sacraments as well.

Growing Awareness

When the initial shock wears off the dying person enters a longer period of readjustment whilst maintaining a definite interest in life. With the awareness of his condition, Colin begins to express various emotions: anger, tears, remorse and a sense of urgency about getting the practical tasks completed as an expression of his anxiety for Anne and the children. We have already discussed many of these feelings in relation to the bereaved.

One new factor is Colin's attempt, through the chaplain, to *bargain* with God for more time. This has been described by Elizabeth Kubler-Ross[1] as one 'stage' in the reactions of dying people which may be revealed to clergy more often than to other people. This is because the dying person may see the minister as a confidential person who will not laugh at their request and their attempt to gain extra time. But the minister is also seen as someone who may be able to persuade God to agree to the request, 'I suppose you couldn't put in a good word upstairs . . .?' often said as a half joke.

Such bargaining is really an attempt to postpone the 'evil hour' and may be linked with feelings of guilt for not having attended church more frequently or given more to charity. Quite often the person will make some promise of a gift of money if they can live until their son or daughter has been married. If you feel ill prepared to meet God face to face then it is not surprising that you should try to postpone the moment. A sensitive approach on the part of the clergyman may uncover some of the underlying guilt feelings and help the person to accept that, whilst bargaining is understandable, it is not a very helpful way of coping in the long term.

The dying have many anxieties and fears to cope with and it is only as one relates sensitively to the dying person that one may learn what these are. Some of these anxieties can be alleviated quite easily, others may prove very difficult.

Fear of the unknown and the importance of hope

In the very early stages of the realization of the nature of his illness Colin wanted information. This information was partly medical, partly nursing, in that he wanted to know about the disease, the treatment and to receive reassurance about the care he would receive in the future and whether he would die in pain. He wanted to know what lay ahead and what the *act* of dying would be like. During this early part of his grieving he was trying to sort out who he could trust with his questions, who would be honest in their answers and who would be honest enough to say, 'I do not know'. If he was going to die, then he was going to do it well!

There were several discussions with the chaplain and with other people concerning death, life after death and the nature of God. Colin was a practising Christian and felt guilty at questioning his beliefs. Nevertheless, he felt that he had to ask himself whether he really believed or was his faith only an intellectual acceptance of a belief system. He felt angry with God but also wondered if his own weak faith had contributed to his being ill. He needed to feel that it was all right to question God and to be angry with him. This is, of course, a feeling that is common to many dying people. Colin found much comfort from reading the Easter narratives and especially the references to Thomas with his doubts and uncertainties and the fact that Thomas was not rejected because he doubted. Tillich's phrase '. . . the courage to accept oneself as accepted in spite of being unacceptable'[2] was to be a key phrase at various points in his illness, because it held out to him the *hope* of being accepted even though at times he felt very unacceptable to God, himself and to his family.

Hope is an essential part of living as well as dying for it is a part of being. Hope involves us in remaining open to what may seem improbable possibilities. For Colin and Anne, apart from the Christian hope of a life after death, there had to be the hope concerning life at present which they expressed in terms of planning a family holiday. They both knew that the holiday would probably not come about, but the main pleasure seemed to be in the planning and the sharing of dreams and fantasy. No firm bookings were made and no money was paid since 'there would always be time to sort that out later'. Although you know that your life expectancy is short, you cannot make that the sole topic of conversation all the time.

Loss of family, friends, self-identity and one's body

Colin was naturally very anxious about his family and how they would cope without him. Together with Anne he tried to sort out the practical issues and, in some ways, seeing that she would cope was both a source of resentment as well as a comfort. Much of the anger that Colin expressed towards his wife stemmed from a resentment that she was well and he was not. He felt angry that his own body had become diseased and had let him down. When illness alters our appearance or our ability to perform the tasks we are used to doing we may experience a loss of self-esteem and self-integrity. Some people may ask for no visitors or a restriction of visitors if they feel this very keenly. A young woman who was dying with a very disfiguring cancer of the jaw felt that her body was visibly disintegrating and was rejecting her. At one point in her illness she asked for no visitors apart from her mother, her husband and the minister who was visiting her because she did not feel that she could cope with other people's reactions to what the disease was doing to her appearance. It was the loving contact with her family and others which helped this young woman to re-establish her self-esteem and to face people again. It was their loving touch which put her in contact with her own body once again and this underlines for us the importance of touch in the process of healing and re-establishment of identity.

Human contact affirms who we are and the dying person needs contact with his or her own self and others right to the last, so that he or she may remain a person and so not be reduced to a number or a case. The process of dying will sometimes awaken submerged feelings of dislike or hatred, as well as feelings of love and tenderness, towards family members and others. It is important to help the dying and their family and friends to understand and accept the variety of, sometimes conflicting, emotions that may arise. The way in which drugs are used will have an effect on how the dying are able to sort out these feelings. In some cultures people will refuse any medication which will cloud their thought because they wish to approach death with a clear mind. In the case of the Buddhist, for example, his next life through reincarnation is dependent upon the quality of his present life and he will not want to spoil it in his last hours. The same can be said for many non-Buddhists.

It is when the dying have been able to reaffirm the nature and value of some of their relationships that they can then achieve a measure of peace which can help them to separate from their loved ones. Another factor which helps them in the separation is a belief in the after-life because it reaffirms the continuity of one's being, and the belief that we will be reunited with those who have already died. In this way, the dying may find comfort in the knowledge that the present separation, painful though it is, is only a temporary one.

The fear of loneliness, pain and suffering

Closely associated with the loss of identity and of one's body is the fear of pain and isolation. If you are ill in bed with a non-fatal illness, such as 'flu, you can feel very isolated in the upstairs bedroom while the family are continuing everyday life downstairs. It can be very tempting to keep banging on the floor in order to be reassured that you have not been forgotten. If you are ill in hospital this feeling can be heightened, especially at visiting times if your visitors are late or are not coming. At one point in his illness Colin accuses his wife of adultery because she always looked 'happy' when visiting and, in his fantasy, she must already be getting used to life without him by having a lover.

In seeking to prevent loneliness one needs to be aware of the danger of never allowing the dying time to be alone! It is a matter of reassuring the dying person that people are available to the extent that he or she needs and desires them to be. In conversing with the dying person it is helpful if we remember not to make their dying the sole focus, but to spend time engaging the person in everyday tasks and interests as far as they wish. In their better moments, the dying need to be able to re-enter the family if we are to avoid the extreme situation that Colin experienced where he had 'died' socially before he died physically.

Many people associate dying with pain and suffering and pray for a 'good, peaceful end'. Pain is an important factor in creating loneliness and isolation. If pain seems to have some purpose or meaning (e.g. the pain experienced following an operation while the wound heals) then we can usually bear it more easily, or at least put up with it. If however the pain is needless or seemingly unnecessary it becomes suffering and cannot usually be borne for long. 'Man is not destroyed by suffering, he is destroyed by suffering without meaning.'[3] The minister of religion may be seen as someone who comes to encourage stoicism and martyrdom. Being involved with life and other people is also an important factor in coping with pain. The control of pain is something requiring a variety of approaches including medication, involvement of other people, information about the causes of the pain, and the involvement of the patients in their own management of pain. Pain and the anticipation of it can very quickly demoralize and is a very important aspect of terminal care, as the Hospice movement has been able to show. It is important that clergy endeavour to liaise with the Macmillan Service (see Appendix B, pp. 138ff) or equivalent home care team within the health district.

Loss of dignity and self-control

Many dying people are afraid that as their illness progresses they will lose control over various bodily functions and therefore also lose some of their dignity. Colin had already suffered hair loss as a result of the drugs he had received and he found it hard to accept that he might become even weaker and more dependent upon others. The loss of independence and control of your body or mind can be a frightening prospect. Although there may be times when it is nice to be allowed to regress and be cared for, after a while it can become very irritating and smothering. If relatives find it satisfying to have 'someone to care for' it can be difficult for them to encourage the sick person towards whatever degree

Letting Go

of independence is possible, and to allow them to make their own decisions about what happens to themselves.

From the beginning Colin made it clear that he wished to maintain a strong measure of control over what was told to him as well as what would happen to his family through the provision of a will and the checking of insurance cover, etc. The relinquishing of responsibility should be a gradual process for most people. In Colin and Anne's case it happened a bit too quickly in that he handed 'everything' over and then failed to die! This could not be foreseen at the time but the feeling of having to be reborn into his family might not have been as acute had Colin retained a greater measure of control for longer. Against this one must say that had Colin died instead of going into remission we might have concluded that it was a 'perfect' resolution with everybody ready and the patient dying on time!

An important prayer for Colin at various times was the prayer for serenity, 'Lord, grant me the courage to accept the things I cannot change, the strength to change the things I can, and the wisdom to know the difference' (Niebuhr).

Resolution — the Final Phase

When talking about the reactions of bereaved people, we described how eventually many of the tensions and conflicts within them are resolved. The same is true for the dying person if he or she has sufficient time and support to cope with these feelings before the moment of death.

One of the most noticeable features of the final phase of dying is the way in which the person gradually withdraws from other people and appears depressed. When one considers the variety of losses experienced by the dying person, prior to the final loss of their own life, it is very natural and not surprising that they should have periods of depression. The depression seems to take two forms:

The first type of depression is that which clearly arises as a result of losses already experienced and is akin to *reactive depression* and will respond very well to reassurance and encouragement. Sometimes drug therapy may be necessary, especially if the experience of loss has had the effect of triggering off any underlying mental illness.

Towards the end of the person's life one often sees a second type of depression which is not the result of past loss but is linked to impending loss. Here one sees depression being used as a tool to prepare for loss and to facilitate acceptance and the final letting go. Sadness may be a better term to use. If *our* anxiety causes us to encourage the dying person to look on the bright side and does not allow them to be sad, then our reassurances will be meaningless and we shall have made it clear that we cannot share this part of the experience with them. On the other hand, if we are able to permit the dying to express sorrow, to be sad, quiet or withdrawn then we shall have done much to ease the isolation of this final phase. 'You didn't say much, but you let me be sad. Thank you.'

This part of dying is marked by its silences, when communication is more non-verbal than verbal, where much more is conveyed by the touch of the hand and a silent sitting together. Too much interruption and interference by relatives and others in an attempt to 'cheer up' the patient will often irritate because it cuts across the person's emotional and spiritual preparation. It is usual for the dying to sleep a great deal at this latter phase and the minister may find that when he visits the person may open his or her eyes, smile, hold the minister's hand, perhaps ask for a prayer or blessing and then drift back into sleep. This, of course, assumes that there has been a good relationship between the dying person and the minister prior to this visit. If the person has an ambivalent feeling about clergy, or reacts to a stereotype image, then to open the eyes and see a minister may have an alarming rather than comforting effect. Although this situation can be dealt with if it happens it is a great help if the minister has been given the opportunity to relate with the dying person long before the terminal stage. Where there has been a long and meaningful relationship the visit of the minister with an appropriate prayer and blessing can bring the release that the person seemed to be waiting for.

A young eighteen-year-old girl who was suffering from leukaemia was readmitted to hospital. Her parish priest, who knew her well, visited her in hospital and, together with the hospital chaplain, anointed her. Over the next few weeks her condition deteriorated and she was visited regularly by the parish priest and hospital chaplain. One evening the chaplain was sitting with her, neither saying very much. As he got up to leave he said that he would see her the next day and, placing his hands on her head, said a short prayer of commendation and blessed her. He turned to leave and as he did so she said, 'Wait'. Then she said 'Goodbye', gave a deep sigh, and died. He felt sure at that time that the prayer, commendation and blessing had led her to feel that now was the time to 'let go'. Such a 'perfect end' is rare and quite often the death occurs when you have just left the person in order to get a cup of tea or post a letter. One should beware of feeling guilty about this and burdening oneself with 'If only . . .'.

The above discussion of the process of dying is derived from the experience of Colin as well as that of other people. However, these reactions, of both the dying and the bereaved, are modified greatly by the circumstances surrounding the death as well as the personalities of the people involved. It is important that the dying should be allowed to die their own death rather than be forced to fit the pattern of behaviour imposed by the hospital, institution or by the expectations of family or society.[4] One of the dangers inherent in trying to describe the process of dying is that people then take the described pattern as the norm and attempt to fit people to it. In so doing we are failing to respond to the dying or the bereaved *where they are*; instead we are reacting to them at the point we feel they should have reached. The problem is that the dying person may not have read the book! We are in the same situation as the mother who becomes worried that her child does not conform to the pattern described in her baby book — the baby has not read the book either. Mother and baby normally, of course, teach each other.

One person who has contributed greatly to our understanding of the reactions of a dying person is Dr Elisabeth Kubler-Ross who interviewed over two hundred terminally ill patients. As a result of these interviews she proposed a model to help us to understand what she described as the various *stages* in coming to terms with our own death: Denial and Isolation, Anger, Bargaining, Depression, Acceptance and Hope.[5]

In describing these different stages Dr Kubler-Ross gives many examples of people who do not follow this sequential process, but it is a very convenient way of classifying what people may be experiencing. Because of this, unfortunately, some people have referred to these stages as a normal sequence of events and inferred that any deviation from this pattern is abnormal. Such does not seem to have been Dr Kubler-Ross's intention. What she was offering was a useful way of identifying people's feelings without dictating a set order. She was not offering people a framework within which the person was allowed to die!

In her autobiography of her own dying experience JoAnn Smith describes her confusion when she realized that she was not following the 'prescribed pattern'. After struggling with this she concludes: 'The stages of dying are not necessarily chronological. In my own experience I have moved back and forth through several of these a number of times.'[6]

Schulz and Aderman[7] conclude that each patient will 'adopt a pattern of behaviour' which persists until death occurs. There may be a lot of similarity in the reactions of different people, however, and there also seems to be much flowing back and forth of these feelings. An analogy that has helped some people is that of the tide. Beachcombers are well aware of the way in which the character of the beach can change with each tide. One day the tide deposits driftwood and seaweed. Another day it deposits dead seabirds, oil or sewage. After another tidal flow the beach may be swept clean of all debris. One cannot be sure from day to day what you will find on the beach. The same would seem to be true of grief. This analogy of the tide flowing back and forth and depositing anger or tears or sadness or cheerfulness seems to reflect the comment made by many people, 'All of a sudden I just became angry, it swept over me'.

In relating with the dying and the bereaved our task would seem to be to be sensitive and try to identify the particular stresses that they are experiencing *at that moment*. Then we should try to respond to the emotions and needs expressed — this will often mean offering practical help (getting the district nurse, doctor, a commode, a night-sitter), or offering emotional support (a box of tissues, a listening ear), or spiritual support (through the ministry of the word and sacraments as seems appropriate). In this way we shall not be imposing upon the dying or the bereaved *our* expectation of how they should

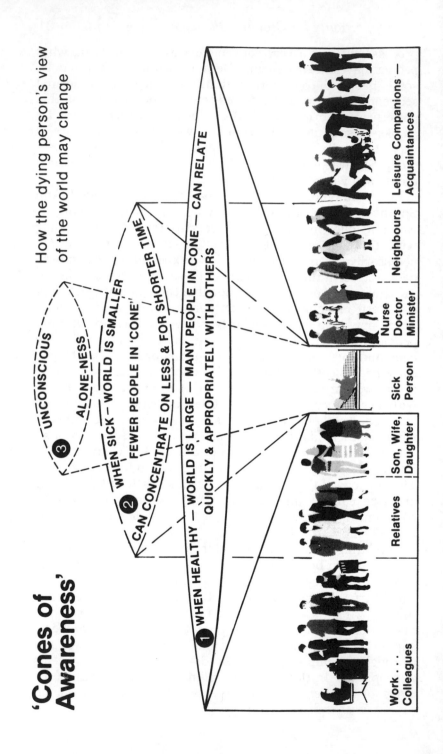

'Cones of Awareness'

How the dying person's view of the world may change

① WHEN HEALTHY — WORLD IS LARGE — MANY PEOPLE IN CONE — CAN RELATE QUICKLY & APPROPRIATELY WITH OTHERS

② CAN CONCENTRATE ON LESS & FOR SHORTER TIME — FEWER PEOPLE IN 'CONE' — WHEN SICK — WORLD IS SMALLER

③ ALONE-NESS — UNCONSCIOUS

Work... Colleagues | Relatives | Son, Wife, Daughter

Sick Person

Nurse Doctor Minister | Neighbours | Leisure Companions — Acquaintances react. Rather, we shall be reacting sensitively to how the person is *actually* feeling. Thus we allow the person to die their own death or to grieve their own grief and in this way we make easier the letting go.

The diagram illustrates three views of the world as a person may experience it during illness and while facing death, whether at home or in hospital. It is set out in a simplified way with many details omitted so that it can be read more clearly. The diagram should not be taken as an exact description of what every terminally ill person experiences. It is essentially a framework which those who are involved with a dying person can use in an attempt to heighten their own understanding of what is happening.[8]

Notes

1. E. Kubler-Ross, *On Death and Dying* (Tavistock, 1970).
2. P. Tillich, *The Courage to Be* (Fontana, 1979), p. 160.
3. Viktor Frankl, *Man's Search for Meaning* (Hodder and Stoughton, 1963).
4. Requests for euthanasia often reflect the feeling that one is not receiving the care that he or she desires. See *On Dying Well* (Church Information Office, 1975).
5. Kubler-Ross, op. cit.
6. JoAnn Kelly Smith, *Free Fall* (SPCK, 1977), p. 48.
7. R. Schulz and D. Aderman, 'Clinical Research and the Stages of Dying', *Omega,* 5 (1974), pp. 137-43.
8. I am very grateful to the Revd Allan Reed, who was Chaplain of Massachusetts General Hospital, Boston, Mass., USA, while I was a Clinical Pastoral Education student there in 1970/71. He first set me thinking about the ideas which have developed into this diagram and the bar chart in chapter 4. (I.A-S.)

THREE

Letting Go

―――

Dragons live for ever, but not so little boys.
 (LAST VERSE OF SONG 'PUFF THE MAGIC DRAGON')

'Pooh! . . . I'm not going to do Nothing any more.'
'Never again?'
'Well, not so much. They don't let you.'[1]

A television film on facing death and bereavement contained
an important sequence which did not involve a funeral or
even interviewing a group of newly bereaved people. An
eighteen-month-old child was filmed playing in the sandpit
with her mother in the park where they went together nearly
every day. On this occasion her mother played with her for a
while and then, whilst the child's attention was engrossed,
left her and walked out of sight. The child subsequently
played on, quite unconcerned, until the moment two or three
minutes later when she realized that her mother had left her.
At first she did not seem particularly concerned. Presumably
she had coped with similar separations before, but when her
mother failed to reappear the child ceased playing altogether
and commenced a search for her mother which became
increasingly desperate. She looked all around her and
anxiously scanned the faces of other mothers with their
children. Eventually she sat alone in the middle of the sandpit
and sobbed uncontrollably. She stopped playing and resisted
vigorously the attempts of any other adults or children to
comfort her. She rocked to and fro and seemed completely
absorbed in herself. Slowly, however, she began to play
again, alone; and after a while she started playing, although
fairly tentatively, with other children.

To a casual observer it looked as though the child was
playing in exactly the same way as before her mother left, but
this was not so. An experienced nursery nurse and mother,

on being shown the film, immediately pointed out the differences in the little girl's way of playing, before and after her separation from her mother. When the child's mother reappeared the little girl ran up to her and hugged her and the reunion was complete. She could, of course, have behaved in other ways, possibly ignoring her mother, apparently punishing her for daring to abandon her. Although unable to express in words how she felt, the child's separation from her mother was the end of her world as she knew it. Her actions and feelings were in fact those which are typically seen in grieving people, children or adults. Much will depend of course on the nature of the loss, the age of the person, and whether the feelings are expressed in actions or words. Freud,[2] interestingly, points out that, to an external observer, bereaved people frequently behave identically to people who in another setting might be labelled 'mad'. Grief, which is not madness but part of the fear which surrounds the process of 'letting go', has to do with the confusion which is so often made between natural and important feelings connected with loss and what are sometimes taken as the manifestations of mental illness.

It is impossible to go far into the story of our individual growth and development without facing the key issues of letting go and being let go. At birth the infant is let go from his mother's womb to face a new world, one which is very different and which may feel hostile and strange. His existence prior to birth has been mainly safe and secure and he and his mother are physically one. Both may feel intensely the experience of separation which takes place at birth and which is, of course, crucial if each is to be a separate person although tied together by genes and a very complex set of emotions. If you are capable of being attached to someone you have also to face the risk and pain of letting go. At birth the baby moves from one existence to the other and if the time and place are right for him and for his mother he will be let go into the loving and caring hands of the doctor or midwife.

But letting go is a double-edged expression. It can imply being drawn gently into a new sort of existence; or being released or dragged into a void where nothing is safe and nothing consistent. At every point of life which involves growth there seems to be a need to look and feel backwards as well as forwards as an essential ingredient in managing the change successfully. Notions which adults take for granted, such as trust, do not come automatically to a young child, or a person facing a crisis like death, whether their own or that of someone close. When a baby is left alone he is incapable of trusting his mother or father to come back to him. Bowlby and others argue that only after the baby has some experience of being left and found again has he some framework against which to judge the world and begin to trust it.[3] (The simple game of Peep-Bo, much enjoyed by adults and babies, is in essence about losing and refinding, albeit in play.) These losses are necessary for the emotional growth of the infant.

It is precisely those feelings about whether it is possible to trust or not, and whether the world is a safe place or not, which we all of us meet in facing death and loss. The loss of a person, of a place, a stage in one's life or even the possible loss of one's self through one's own death, raise the possibility yet again of how safe it is to trust. Frequently people who are facing their own death, or the loss of a close friend or relation, will describe how their trust in themselves and in people close to them, and even in God, has been profoundly shaken by what has happened. The experience of loss is rather like losing the 'map' of our world which we have built up throughout our lives, and after every change it has to be built again but differently. This is not something which most of us manage by thinking about it. It seems to stem from our early experience of loss and how we have coped with it.

Many adults can describe vividly their first day at school, memories of which usually involve the loss of home and so many things connected with early childhood, rather than the benefits subsequently discovered! Altruism or a conscious encouragement of the child to think on the bright side and on the benefits which he is about to achieve have a limited value. It is very difficult to reassure any child or adult who does not feel some basic assurance on the basis of earlier losses and separations which have been painful but eventually tolerable. In the case of going to school, the separation involves both the child and the parents. There may be some mutual reluctance to let go and to be let go. (A teacher once commented to one of the authors that there was rarely a homesick child without a childsick parent!) It has been the experience of hospital staff that many people describe their admission to hospital as very similar to their first day at school.

A child who has a younger brother or sister born into the family, however well prepared for the event, will never have exactly the same position in his family again. He may have abandoned the position of youngest child in the family, one with benefits and disadvantages. His only way of coping with the future may be to behave like the child he used to be. This process is sometimes called 'regression', going back in feelings and behaviour, to a way of coping which belongs to an earlier stage of life, when the outside world feels intolerable. It is one very important way of coping with loss which we shall encounter again.

The Christian Church, along with other world religions, often has contact with people during the times when their lives may be undergoing great change, e.g. when babies are born, at puberty, marriage and when sickness and death become part of life. Pastoral care is particularly concerned with offering support, comfort and meaning to people who are undergoing change in their lives. In an important book, Clebsch and Jaekle[4] outline the historical background of some of the functions which are now taken for granted in pastoral care. They point out that one important element of care in the early Christian Church, in the time of persecution, was quite simply to offer the means for surviving and hanging on, the work of *sustaining*. Later came the issue of *reconciling* those who had fallen away under persecution. Whilst the historical context is clearly different, the themes of sustaining and reconciling remain crucially important. It is deceptively easy to think that change produces quite straightforward feelings: gladness when something happens which is perceived as pleasant; and sadness when, for example, sickness or death occur. Feelings connected with change and loss are usually not quite so simple. Good care may consist of listening to, recognizing and understanding, words and feelings which may be contrary to the publicly expressed spirit of the occasion. To quote two examples:

1. A young man recently married went to see his minister

because he felt that after six months of marriage he could not understand why he felt so trapped and sometimes quite sad in a partnership with a much loved wife. The minister, instead of encouraging him to think about what he had gained and how lucky he was, asked him what he thought he had lost when he got married. He began to talk with feeling about having lost his bearings. As he put it, 'The me I have had to live with until I got married has gone. I am never going to be the same again'. He found it was of immeasurable value to face the experience of loss and change as part of his adjustment to a marriage which he wanted very much to succeed.

2. A woman in her late fifties, whose husband died suddenly, was visited by a friend who kept mentioning how much she must have lost and how much she would miss her 'dear husband'. The newly-widowed woman became much distressed and later confided, to the minister, that the marriage had been a difficult one and that, although she missed her husband terribly in many ways, she wondered whether God would ever forgive her, for her immediate feelings on hearing of his death were ones of relief.

Every stage of growth carries with it the possibility of both benefit and threat. This was well described by a mother who, after the birth of her baby, exclaimed after a few, trying days, 'Will there be anything of me left?'—a sentiment which many would echo, not just in a maternity ward nor just connected with motherhood. H. A. Williams[5] describes death not just in terms of a physical body ceasing to function but also as the giving up of control, something which happens at many points in life. Giving up control is sometimes described as a 'little death' and can involve both a change in relationships, but also be part of the adjustment, for example, to a body which functions very differently after severe illness, accident or mutilating surgery, or even to the changed person who emerges from the experience.[6] The experience of sleep is frequently connected with death and is sometimes offered as an euphemism for it, frequently to the dismay of those who may connect sleep with death, especially if they have learnt prayers like, 'If I die before I wake, I pray the Lord my soul to take'.

So far, we have been looking mainly at those crises which are a normal part of our growth and which can to some extent be predictable. But there are other crises in life which Caplan[7] describes as 'accidental'. A child's pet may die. How his parents and other adults help him with the crisis may affect profoundly the way in which he copes with other crises later in life. 'The child, when he first discovers that people die, quickly draws out the personal implications of the fact and, although in most incidences the effect of the original shock quickly disappears before the pressure of more immediate interest, the fact is duly registered by the mind and realisation of its fuller significance steadily grows.'[8]

Adults may seek to shield the child at all costs from the reality of death, even, in the case of a pet, to the extent of buying an identical animal in the hope that the child's pain can be alleviated or avoided, all in the belief that the child will be fooled by the deception. The child might be given an alternative explanation of the loss, the pet 'has gone away' or even 'gone to be with Jesus'. Studies made of explanations that parents give to their children about death suggest that 'religious' explanations are used almost as frequently by those parents who claim they have no religious belief as by those who claim religious allegiance.[9] The need to protect children from pain runs deep in the instincts of most adults. Children's literature, however, gives some evidence that it is fantasy rather than reality which is often hardest to cope with. (The story of *Beauty and the Beast* describes how the heroine faces up to her promise to marry the Beast, only to find that the Beast has become a prince. The fantasy of marriage to the old and ugly gives way to the excitement of the real person she discovers.) Pets may have, among their other important functions, that possibility of introducing children, and sometimes adults, to the experience of loss and grief in a painful but safe way when the pet dies. Terrible as the loss of a pet may be, it would normally be much less terrible in its implications than, say, the loss of a parent, brother, sister or friend. Many children seem to have strong instincts about doing the right thing around such events. One twelve-year-old put it, 'The other day I saw a fox in the road and it was dead and we drove past it. That's wrong. You should always stop and say goodbye to dead things.'

Hospital staff, funeral directors and ministers may frequently meet people who in the middle of their life have not encountered death at first hand or even seen a dead body. But the way in which losses other than death are faced may be crucial, partly as an experience of living and maturing, and also as a struggling to understand the final loss which is one's own death.

Other losses can feel like a death or a series of 'little deaths'.

Michael had a stroke for which he was treated in hospital and which necessitated his leaving his managerial job and sitting at home. He became dependent on other people and he found it very hard to live with a body which, as he put it, 'no longer behaved'. He lost his status as a working person, as an active man, since he had to rely on his wife and daughter for much of his physical care, and he once described his experience as being a 'thousand-stage death'. He felt very strongly that his physical death was the last stage in a process and that he had been forced to let go his life in little bits over the previous two years.

Janet underwent extensive heart surgery and when she later came home told her friends and her minister that, whilst in hospital, she had had to face for the first time in her life the possibility of her own death and the knowledge that her body was not infallible. She had found this devastating since she had set great store by keeping herself healthy and making herself look attractive. She said, 'It was very hard for me to accept having to live in a body which was so diseased,' but she also saw her own coming close to death as something which made her rethink her life in terms of what was and what was not important.

Dorothy, a woman in her thirties with two pre-school children, entered hospital for the removal of a lump on her breast and found that, when she recovered consciousness, the breast had been removed. For two days she refused to mention what had happened and would not even look down at the site of the operation. However, she broke down in tears soon after her return home and told her husband to leave her since she was no longer, as she put it, 'a proper woman'. In challenging him she seemed to be asking him to do the thing which she most dreaded. She subsequently described the loss of her breast as like 'the beginning of the end'. She and her husband, with much support from friends, both came to recognize that their relationship would never be quite the same again and that it had to accommodate both the loss which had happened to her and the fact that she was suffering from a malignant illness.

Frequently, the treatment of some illnesses will involve the use of drugs, radiotherapy or surgery, which may alter very dramatically a person's physical appearance. A person may put on or lose weight, or their distribution of hair may change. A woman receiving treatment remarked that what had affected her most had been to look at herself in the mirror and to see, as she put it, all the hair in the wrong place. Sometimes the feelings which are connected with the change that illness or accident may bring about are described as 'change of body image'. Not only may the outside world appear a very different place and one's 'map' of that be changed, but more fundamentally, one's ability to live in one's own body may be considerably affected. There are no rigid rules about what one person may feel for no two people will have identical feelings about the same experience. But some sick people will experience frequent examination and medication, for example, as losing control over their own bodies which may assume as much importance as the illness itself. This need not necessarily apply just to people who are terminally ill or facing serious illness.

Jane had a long history of miscarriages and realized that she would probably never be able to give birth to her own child. She described very vividly how she went through two or three days when she was thoroughly disgusted with her own body. She could not even bear to look at herself in the mirror since she felt so empty and useless. She did not like her husband to look at her either.

Such feelings usually pass, but it is important that they can be shared, if the person wishes. Most frequently help is best given by listening rather than trying to change the way someone else should cope. What most people dread is that their behaviour, following such losses, may be seen as 'irrational', whereas it is a very common expression of pain and confusion. Of course, the confusion may be felt by the sick person's friends and family as well, but possibly slightly differently. If a key person in a family, like a mother, becomes ill her role can never be filled but her husband, relatives, friends and children may find themselves doing things to which they are not accustomed. She may simultaneously welcome the relief and also feel that her family may be managing too well without her, and she may experience resentment that she is no longer needed. Sometimes, if a person is ill for a long time, they may feel excluded from the family and feel that their role has been taken over by others. A man who, like Colin (in chapter 2), is ill over a long period may feel very cut off from the rest of his family as they begin to take over the jobs he did at home and may also feel that he has lost his position as father and provider. Sometimes, in concentrating attention on a sick person, the needs of those close to him to grieve the loss involved in his sickness may not be so obvious, and only appear suddenly and sometimes quite dramatically.

> Graham, a young man paralysed after a road accident, was in hospital and a rehabilitation centre for ten months and his wife had visited him faithfully during that time. It was only on the day that he was discharged that she said very quietly as if she was not sure whether she could be heard or not, 'And will someone tell me what sort of a man they are giving me back'.

Her outburst was concerned, rightly, with herself and the profound changes, emotional, physical and sexual, which were implicit in her husband's condition. Very few of us live in such isolation that the effect of loss is confined to one person.

The 'little deaths' we have been describing provide part of the framework in which wider losses can be faced later on in life. They are not an exact preparation but to go through them successfully is to provide a framework against which larger and more fundamental losses can be faced.

Notes

1. A. A. Milne, *The House at Pooh Corner* (Methuen, 1928).
2. Sigmund Freud, 'Mourning and Melancholia' in *Complete Psychological Works of Sigmund Freud*, vol. xiv (1914-16), (Hogarth).
3. J. Bowlby, *Attachment and Loss*, vol. i: *Attachment* (Penguin, 1971).
4. W. A. Clebsch and C. R. Jaekle, *Pastoral Care in Historical Perspective* (Harper and Row, New York, 1967).
5. H. A. Williams, *Four Last Things* (Mowbray, 1960).
6. P. W. Speck, *Loss and Grief in Medicine* (Bailliere Tindall, 1978).
7. G. Caplan, *An Approach to Community Mental Health* (Tavistock, 1969).
8. S. G. F. Brandon, *Man and his Destiny in Great Religions* (Manchester University Press, 1962).
9. G. Gorer, *Death, Grief and Mourning in Contemporary Britain* (Darton, Longman and Todd, 1965).

FOUR

The Context of Dying

The Death of a Baby

Mary H. came into the hospital for a normal delivery of her first baby. During the delivery of her baby she noticed that the atmosphere seemed to have changed and that the staff who were looking after her were rather different in their attitude. She did not feel able at the time to ask what was happening, but she sensed that something was wrong. She was placed in a side room in the maternity ward by herself. She wondered why, and asked her husband why she had not been able to see the baby.[1] It was only then that her husband told her that the baby had been born dead. Her first reaction was not to believe it and she insisted that the hospital had somehow confused the babies. Slowly the reality of what had happened dawned on her and she began to wonder why she had been so punished.

The birth of a baby who fails to survive is a much less common occurrence than it used to be, so that a still-birth, or the death of a baby in the first few days of life is a shattering and unexpected event. Mrs H. was not even sure whether her baby could have a funeral or not and she did not know how to approach a clergyman. The experience of losing a child early on in its life has been described by one parent as 'death before life' and it is against all the normal established order. Most of us expect to be survived by our children rather than to survive them.

In Mrs H.'s case, she was much helped by being taken to see the body of her baby. Some parents certainly do not want to do that. For parents like Mr and Mrs H. the emotive experience of seeing the body of their baby gave them the opportunity of what one mother called 'seeing rather than wondering'. Fantasy about what might be is often more frightening than the reality of what is actually there. Some units in hospitals where premature or seriously ill babies are nursed will routinely offer parents a photograph of their baby. (Some even have a closed-circuit television linking the mother's bedside with the nursery.) If the baby lives the photograph provides the mother with some idea of how her baby is when she may not be in a position to see it; and if the baby dies it may be a crucial reminder to the parents that they did have a child with an existence of its own. A mother of a still-born baby described how confused she felt since it was hard to live with the memory of her pregnancy, the physical signs that her body was giving her,[2] contrasted with the fact that she had no baby in her arms. It was as if, she said, nine important months of her life had never happened, but she knew they had, and later she needed time to think about them and talk about them.

Mourning may not just be about things that have happened in the past but can equally involve possibilities which have not yet been realized. It is not uncommon for the parents of still-born babies and those who die soon after birth to experience profound feelings of self-disgust, as if somehow they had failed as parents and as people.[3]

Mrs H. and her husband finally contacted their local minister who readily agreed to their request for a funeral for the baby. The service was simple and it was a sad occasion, but for the parents it seemed to recognize the fact that their baby's life had been a real one and that the 'chapter had been properly closed'. Even if a child is still-born he has still had an existence before his birth. The mother will usually have felt its movements inside her. Most Christian churches have now responded to our increased understanding of the nature of the life a baby leads before birth by being quite prepared to offer a funeral for a baby if this is what the parents wish.[4]

The sudden death of a baby at home, often in its cot and usually at a time when the parents are not present, is usually described as the 'cot death syndrome'.[5] The parents will usually have had some chance to get to know the baby and to incorporate it into the life of the family. He will have become a real and important person for his brothers and sisters and other relatives. In legal terms a cot death is a sudden and unexplained death for which, as a matter of routine, the police must be called and the coroner informed. Most police officers and coroner's staff handle the investigation of cot deaths with great sensitivity, but the legal requirements may frequently compound the parents' sense of failure, that their ability as parents is somehow being questioned. A father whose baby died suddenly at home said, 'I had not realized that I would have to make a statement to the police. It was very illogical, but I kept thinking that they were going to ask me whether I had attacked the child. I felt so guilty and I knew that my wife did too. But at the time it was impossible to talk about.' Because of the circumstances in which most deaths of babies occur, it is extremely important to try to avoid, as far as possible, any approach which may sound as if the parents and the family are being judged, for most people in these circumstances feel guilty enough already.

There is a natural tendency if something terrible happens to think back on what one might have done to bring this about. One mother was terrified to mix the feed of her new baby because she felt that maybe she had not got the mixture quite right for her previous baby who had died inexplicably in his cot. Some women may well experience a miscarriage early in pregnancy as a 'little bereavement'. It is usually of scant comfort to someone who has gone through the experience of a miscarriage to be told that it was early in their pregnancy so it could not have meant much. Here again, the issue involved is the facing of lost possibilities in a crisis. Most of us do not think logically especially when we are under stress. One task of pastoral care may be gently to support people who, for example, are connecting things they have done or thought in the past with some loss in the present. 'Is it something I've done?'[6]

The Abnormal Baby

Occasionally children are born with some sort of abnormality. This can involve a condition like a harelip or squint which can be corrected surgically, or a severe congenital disorder such as Spina Bifida or Down's Syndrome (mongolism). The parents of a child who is severely handicapped have to face a double dilemma. It would be hard to imagine a parent wanting or anticipating the birth of a handicapped child. They have to face the loss, in the birth of their other than perfect child, of the perfect child who might have been. This can involve a lot of pain, in struggling to accept a child who is less than perfect, so the task of mourning may be two-fold.

Sometimes the feelings will be too profound to talk about and not everybody uses a framework of words to express them. The services which Christians offer round the birth of children, which mainly strike the theme of thanksgiving, may sometimes be used by parents of handicapped children as part of their way of coping with what has happened. A woman who had given birth to a severely handicapped baby asked for a thanksgiving service for his birth but turned up for the service dressed in black. The minister used a form of service with her which both thanked God for the birth of her child but also contained some prayers which picked up the theme of questioning God and how hard it was to accept something or somebody who was not exactly what was envisaged. Letting go of the image of the perfect child may be crucial for the parents, involving as it does facing their own limitations, before they can make any full acceptance of the child they have.

Death by Suicide

On occasions ministers may find themselves in contact with those who have survived a suicide attempt and also with the relatives and friends of someone who has succeeded in killing themselves. It is not within the scope of this book to discuss in detail the pastoral care of the person who makes a suicide attempt. Interestingly, people who are terminally ill seem to have a low rate of suicide. Whether this is to do with life appearing very sweet if one is terminally ill or whether it is difficult for a seriously ill person to get hold of the means for killing themselves is a matter of some debate. Certainly, impulsive feelings about suicide seem common in some bereaved people, as part of their reaction to the crisis. Sometimes a person may attempt to take their life in the wake of a bereavement. Care of the people who survive when a family member or friend has committed suicide involves taking seriously the very powerful mixed feelings which often follow suicide.

Mrs R., a woman in her late thirties, found out after her
husband's death that he had killed himself. She was both
devastated that he could have done this to her as well as
partly furious with herself for somehow making it happen.
She felt that possibly, if she had been kinder or more understanding, her husband's death would not have happened.

The funeral service for her husband was important for
her and the vicar tried to provide a service which picked up
in its themes the very mixed feelings, as she put it 'of being
either the murderer or being murdered', which she felt.

The feeling that something more might have been done seems
particularly to pervade survivors when someone has committed suicide.

Some of the most difficult family situations one can imagine
may involve the care of a family where one member makes a
suicide attempt which will eventually lead to their death, but
not immediately.

Mrs X., during a quarrel with her husband, swallowed
weedkiller which was a slow-acting poison and she survived
her attempted suicide for three days. During that time her
husband and children alternated between wanting to go in
to her hospital ward and cry with her and tell her that they
forgave her, and getting very angry with the hospital who
could not save her, and with the minister because God had
not stopped her taking the poison. The situation was never
completely resolved but the woman's daughter at her
funeral commented that the 'poison was in the whole
family'. With much support from friends and neighbours
the family members began very slowly to be clearer about
what responsibility was properly theirs, and what was the
mother's.

Death in Childhood and Adolescence

For a person to die after the first six weeks of life is not now a
common event. The circumstances in which a child or young
person dies, at a time when he may 'have everything to look
forward to', and frequently as a result of an accident or

sudden illness, may make a particular and unforgettable impact on those who are involved.

Michael P. was an eighteen-year-old man driving his fiancée home in his first car. They were involved in a crash in which his fiancée was killed instantly and Michael was taken to hospital seriously injured. During the time that his fiancée's funeral was taking place he was in the hospital's intensive care unit undergoing plastic surgery and his jaws were wired together. He afterwards said that, although he knew that his fiancée had died, it was still unreal for him. His friends visited him in hospital and afterwards when he was at home. They did not talk much together about the accident but at one moment thought of buying a plaque to place at the crematorium in the fiancée's memory, and at the next planning their football programme for the next season. It seemed as if nobody knew quite how the fiancée could be mentioned. Michael spent a lot of time sitting by himself and wondering why he had survived the crash when his fiancée had been killed. The health visitor who knew the family and the minister of his local church visited Michael regularly and showed that they understood his need to be angry at times with the other motorist involved, with himself for not having been more careful and for surviving his fiancée, and with the hospital who had not managed to revive her. By the time Michael had recovered he found it very difficult to make contact with his fiancée's parents but finally did so.

Adolescence is hardly ever an easy time for parents or for children and the sudden death of an adolescent child at a time when family life is often stormy can leave a very serious gap and many issues unresolved.

A mother of an adolescent boy killed in a motor-cycle accident bitterly reproached herself for the number of times that she had complained about pieces of motor cycle being left in the house and wondered whether, if she had been more accommodating, her son might have made a better repair on his motor cycle which might then have prevented the accident. Her son's youth club leader who knew him well helped her by remarking casually one day that he really had been a nuisance at times but that he was remembered in the club as a human being with strengths and weaknesses. The mother and father were slowly able to remember their son with the warmth of the relationship and also the difficulties in it.

There are conventions around grief which include the assumption that the dead person was always perfect, so it becomes impossible to speak anything but good of them. The reasons for the convention are quite clear and are rooted in the need to have something good by which to remember the dead person. But, equally, grieving involves putting together a set of memories of the person which bears some resemblance to the way that person was in life.

Children do not usually use a sophisticated system of words to describe their feelings and their world, and children who are terminally ill or bereaved are no exception. One small boy who had a tumour which was not responding to treatment was asked by his mother how he felt. He had certainly not been told that he was going to die but he immediately drew a tank with a little figure floating in front of its gun barrel. 'That's me,' he said. Caring for a child in a long terminal illness is one of the most exhausting and demanding tasks which can come the way of parents, brothers and sisters, other family members and those who have the professional care of the child.[7]

Mark G., a boy of twelve, was admitted to hospital after the onset of severe headaches and was diagnosed with a brain tumour. During the last year of his life he spent some time at home with periods in hospital. He seemed to realize the serious nature of his illness and he made quite sure before his final admission to the hospital that his model cars and his Scout uniform went to people about whom he cared.

Samantha S., a little girl of seven, was admitted to hospital and soon afterwards sent home after an untreatable bone cancer had been diagnosed. The information was given to the parents who did not discuss it with any other family members. Again she attended hospital for treatment. During the time that she was at home her mother found that she begrudged time spent with her other children and made a point of never being far away from Samantha. The other children in the family, who were older, remained outwardly well-behaved but showed other signs that they were resenting their mother's preoccupation with their sister. (Her elder sister said to a visitor that she would like to be ill too, since sick children saw more of grown-ups.) Samantha's father insisted that she was not ill at all and that, if only the family could be rehoused and the children's damp bedroom changed, all would be well. Eventually the mother's and father's marriage broke down and the father coped by failing to visit Samantha in hospital and refusing to attend her funeral. He could, it seemed, only cope by rejecting the situation out of hand and Samantha's mother could only manage by involving herself totally with her daughter's care. It was as if the two parents between them were showing in their actions two extremes, of either getting so involved with a dying child that every other activity goes by the board or by denying the seriousness of what is happening. To try to find a middle way between the two extremes is very hard.

Because the pressures involved in caring for children facing death are so considerable, some attention has been given to the establishment of a hospice for children. Helen House in Oxford aims to provide a pioneer service in caring for terminally ill children in which the needs of the children, their families and the staff who care for them can be sustained.

Development of a Concept of Death

Children may also be involved in the mourning for a member of their family. Sometimes this will be a brother or sister or parent. The way in which children slowly develop the idea of being dead and of death has been explored by Sylvia Anthony in an important study.[8] Small children seem to have very little conception of the permanence of death and are quite capable of talking at one moment about someone having died and at the next moment the possibility of their return.

Janet, a four-year-old, whose brother had died suddenly aged eighteen months, said quite simply, 'John is dead and we've buried him in the ground, but next spring we're going to find him.'

The sort of words used by children like Janet can be surprising for adults who may have seen her earlier, apparently much affected by the death of her brother.

Slowly, the growing child seems to achieve some awareness of the permanence of death. If children lose grandparents and relatives it may be important for them to have a chance to attend the funeral. Adults can often remember in later life occasions in their childhood when, in retrospect, they knew that a family funeral was taking place but at the time their attention had been diverted by a family outing, for example. It is often assumed that the worst thing that could possibly happen for a child would be to see parents and other relied-upon adults apparently deeply affected by mourning. But strangely enough, it may often be the denial of mourning in adults that children find most difficult to handle.

A mother of two young children whose husband had died on the way to work refused to discuss the father's death with her children and told them simply that he had 'gone away'. The children subsequently in their play with other children in their neighbourhood mentioned that their Mummy had cut their Daddy up and put him in little pieces in the ground.

However much adults may feel that they should remain strong 'because of the children', a child's experience of an adult who is sad and devastated but in the long run will be all right is usually much more realistic and reassuring than a blank denial of anything having happened.

Sudden Death

There are clearly occasions when death is unprepared for, when somebody dies after an accident or sudden illness, such as a heart attack. In nearly all such cases feelings of *denial* are likely to be very important. 'I can't believe it's happened. I only saw him two hours ago.'⁹ 'When we last spoke she was laughing and joking.' Frequently the feelings involved in the loss seem to take some time to catch up with the events, especially if a person dies in hospital. His friends and relatives may express bewilderment, frustration, sometimes rage, that more could not have been done. Again, there seems to be some evidence for thinking that those who have been involved in the care of the person in hospital in some way, even if only by sitting by the bedside or talking to an apparently unconscious person, seem to have some experience on which they can draw when looking back. The nursing staff in several intensive care units which treat patients with serious head injuries make a point of encouraging relatives to become involved with basic nursing tasks like lifting and washing the patient to help combat feelings of inadequacy.[10]

A three-year-old child was admitted to the hospital's intensive care unit following a road-traffic accident. She was placed on a life-support machine but was subsequently diagnosed as 'brain dead'. Her mother said, 'If only I could take her home. I feel so helpless.' She was not really asking to take her child home, but, staff believed, for permission to cuddle her. Her mother sat in a chair whilst the doctor, ward sister and chaplain helped lift the child off the bed (complete with tubes) onto her lap where she subsequently 'died'. The mother later said, 'She came into the world with a cuddle and went out with one. That was right.'

In the aftermath of an accident where several people may have died together, much of the mourning and feelings of grief may be expressed by individual people and also by families together. Having some shared experience may be a very powerful bond between people experiencing grief, but it is also not always the case that any two people, let alone any two families or groups of friends, will attach the same importance to similar events and the danger exists that someone may feel deviant and odd, either because they are being very 'hard and unfeeling' or by crying too much and being 'selfish'. There are two aspects of grieving, public and private. The *public* aspect includes going through and facing the public occasions like funerals, requiems, memorial services and so on. Where a major disaster takes place there is universally a sense of outrage and of the things which may not have been done properly and adequately. Much emphasis will frequently be placed on the funeral, memorial service and the social occasion which accompanies it, and if these are ways through which the bereaved can express their feelings and if the outside community (neighbours, distant friends and acquaintances, and sometimes national or civic figures) are involved, this can be a very powerful, and sometimes quite healing, expression of pain and loss. But the other task, as indicated by Lindemann,[11] is a more *private* one. There will be many memories and experiences of the dead person which will not be expressed in a public event like a funeral, and the facing and experiencing of memories, good and bad, and making some sort of whole from which the future can make sense, is a very personal experience (see chapter 5). Both tasks are important, and the minister and others may need to recognize the importance that needs to be given to each. Survivors of a disaster that is publicly reported and widely known about may be prevented by the public expressions of mourning from facing their private grief.[12]

Death in Old Age

Mr and Mrs T. had been married for fifty-two years and they still remembered and spoke warmly of their golden wedding which had been attended by their children and grandchildren. Mr T. used to make them both a cup of tea every morning and on the morning of his wife's death he had gone downstairs to make the tea and when he came back found that his wife was not breathing. He described his first feelings as 'just not being able to believe it'. The family doctor was called and confirmed that Mrs T. had died suddenly in her sleep. The doctor had suggested that the local vicar should be contacted and although Mr T. said he was 'not a churchgoer' he agreed to this. In the meantime, two neighbours had come and had laid out Mrs T.'s body. Mr T.'s reaction on seeing his wife's body was to say quite simply, 'It is her but it is not her'. His children arrived during the day. They lived in an adjacent suburb and wondered whether Mr T. was 'up to' arranging

a funeral and were very concerned to take the burden of
practical arrangements from him. They asked the family
doctor to prescribe a sedative for Mr T. which he refused
but said that, if after a week or so Mr T. had difficulty
sleeping, he would be happy to prescribe something to help
him sleep. Mr T.'s children were also very anxious that he
should leave the house immediately and live with them. He
was very reluctant to leave the house that he had shared
with his wife for forty-two years and said that he wanted to
be with his memories for a while. He said that, although he
knew she was dead, he expected to see her come downstairs
at any time. (Such feelings are common.) The minister
came on the day of Mrs T.'s death and, unlike the
expectations that he would say a lot that was comforting,
he listened to Mr T. and asked him about the early stages
of their marriage, where and how they met, and Mr T. soon
found that he was talking about events that were well in
the past but which he remembered with surprising vivid-
ness, even to details of the dress that Mrs T. was wearing
when they first met. He found it comforting to be put in
touch once again with happy memories.

Mr T. attended his wife's funeral and lived for a while
with his daughter but insisted that he could look after
himself at home. Two years after Mrs T.'s death he kept a
place in the house that he described as her special place
and a time of each day in which he remembered her there.
The minister stayed in frequent contact with him and a lay
visitor from the parish went in to see him every week or so.

It is very easy to assume that an elderly person has 'had a
good life' and to offer this as a comfort to their relatives. But
by the same token, if a person has lived for a long time, they
may have become a key person in the lives of many people
who will not have known life without them. In Mr T.'s case,
his wife had been part of his life for all but twenty years of it.

Grief Work

The process of grieving, as we have suggested, has similar
features whatever the nature of the loss. But the circumstances in which the loss occurs, and other events in the life

of the people involved, may highlight particular aspects. The importance of seeing the loss in the wider context of the person's life span is illustrated in the bar chart entitled 'Grief Work'. This chart follows the way in which in an imaginary situation a wife experiences her grief when her husband dies. It sets out the important landmarks in her life and suggests how grieving for her husband may involve her recalling and re-examining those landmarks.

We have envisaged Mrs K. in late middle-age, with grown-up children and grandchildren. Mr K. was of a similar age to his wife and he has just died suddenly in hospital. On being told of her husband's death Mrs K.'s first reaction may be a denial, 'He can't be dead, I only saw him a short time ago.' Her 'if onlys', perhaps wondering whether things might have been different had, for example, she not left the ward briefly or if a particular nurse had been on duty, are typical of those expressed by many people, especially as they begin to grasp the full impact of what has happened.

All she may be able to do is to keep repeating how good a husband he was, possibly expressing open bewilderment or anger that such a thing could happen to someone who was so good. She may ask why it has happened in a way which is more likely to be a statement of her pain and confusion than a question that has to be answered. If she is given the opportunity to see her husband's body, and accepts this, she may be able to make some distinction between the husband she remembers and the reality of his death. She may well say something like, 'Yes, it is him, but he isn't there'. The diagram shows that as time goes on she seems to be talking and thinking about events which increasingly give rise to memories from her past. Although it may seem to those with her that this is happening in a very random way, and indeed others may try to stop her becoming 'upset', there is more of a pattern to her feelings than appears at first encounter. We would *not* wish to say that our diagram gives a universal method or 'technique', but we are continually struck by the number of people we meet whose grief seems to develop in a way which parallels Mrs K.'s.

The present time in the diagram is marked by the first vertical column on the left. Everything Mrs K. remembers from her past will inevitably come back to the present and

'Grief Work' Illustration

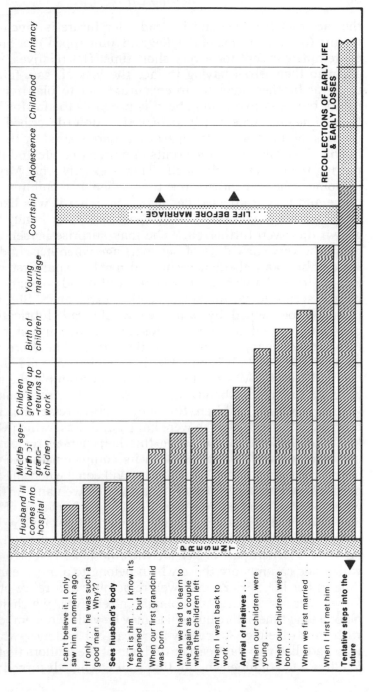

the fact that her husband is dead. Her future is much too
unsure (or in the terms of the diagram 'unmapped') for her to
contemplate except for a very short time. Her relatives, who
are also themselves having to face the loss of, say, father,
uncle or brother, may try to encourage her to plan for the
future but even two hours ahead is probably too far for Mrs
K. to imagine. One newly bereaved widow described the
process of looking at the past she had shared with her
husband as 'taking out the events of our shared life and then
putting them back on the shelf'. This is exactly what Mrs K.
is doing. She remembers the time when her children left
home and how it affected her marriage, what it was like to
begin working outside the home again when her family had
grown up. Even further back she may surprise herself and
recall the very early days of her marriage when her children
were babies and also when she and her husband first met.
For her to recall these events will be painful and poignant but
it also seems to be for her a healing experience. She will
probably be helped by what we would call 'lubricating'
questions (e.g. I don't think you told me where you first met?)
rather than 'change of gear' questions (e.g. Where are you
going to live now?). It is possible that the marriage may have
been difficult for Mrs K. at some point, for example she may
have felt that her husband had an unsatisfactory relationship
with one of their children. She may wish to remember and
talk about the times which were happy and those which were
less than perfect, and by doing this help herself remember
her husband and her marriage in its completeness. As she
relives the events of her life the point will come when she will
naturally remember, when she was a young woman, the time
when her husband entered her life. The early events of her
life, infancy, childhood and adolescence, did not involve her
husband. It may well be that until, very slowly, she can 're-
own' the married part of her life the emotional resources on
which she can rely are those which belong to a much earlier
time in her life. Mrs K. may well remember and relive other
losses, deaths of parents, siblings or relatives, which took
place a long time before but which may be vividly remembered
with much feeling. A seventy-five year old widower whose
wife had died two days earlier told one of the authors that he
felt 'like a lad of nineteen, but that's all wrong!'. It turned out

that this had indeed been his age when he had met his wife. Not every bereaved person speaks of such feelings but they have been common enough in our experience to justify mentioning them.

Only when Mrs K. has gone back over her life and remembered, even re-experienced, some of its most crucial events, may she be able to make her first tentative steps into the future. In the interests of simplicity our diagram tabulates the course of feelings which, of course, never take place quite so neatly! The bereaved person's age, sex, cultural background, previous experiences of loss and the nature of their relationship to the dead person are all variable factors (see chapters 1 and 3). There may be other reasons (see chapter 6) which may delay or may inhibit mourning. Grief may also be inhibited or facilitated by the appropriate use of ritual and an understanding of the cultural setting.

Notes

1. J. Cooper. 'Reactions to Stillbirth: End this Conspiracy of Silence', *Nursing Mirror*, 149, 23 (1979), pp. 31-3.
2. A mother whose baby dies or is stillborn will undergo exactly the same physiological (and most of the psychological) reactions as if she had given birth to a live baby (e.g. the secretion of milk). She will usually be prescribed a course of tablets to suppress lactation.
3. Health Education Council pamphlet, *Loss of your Baby*.
4. If the baby is born in hospital, the parents can be offered a choice whether they arrange a funeral of their own or whether they wish the health authority to take over this function (see ch. 5, p. 76).
5. L. Clapp and J. Price, 'A Review of Sudden Infant Death Syndrome', *Journal of Nursing Care* (March 1980), pp. 13-17, 24.
6. P. W. Speck, 'Easing the Pain and Grief of Stillbirth', *Nursing Mirror* (25 May 1978).
7. Lindy Burton (ed.), *Care of the Child Facing Death* (Routledge, 1974).
8. Sylvia Anthony, *The Discovery of Death in Childhood and After* (Penguin, 1971).
9. See bar chart on p. 57.
10. P. W. Speck, 'The Hospital Visitor', *Nursing Times* (5 July 1973).
11. E. Lindemann, 'Symptomatology and Management of Acute Grief', *American Journal of Psychiatry* (October 1944).
12. A powerfully argued paper, 'Wounds of the Fathers' (H. A. Barocas and C. B. Barocas, *International Review of Psychoanalysis*, 6 (1979), pp. 331ff.), describes the private grief of concentration camp survivors, for whom no public expression or recognition of the enormity of the

Holocaust was ever possible. But the next generation, the survivors' children who had been born after the war, seemed to display the symptoms of their parents' unexpressed grief. See also J. G. Edwards, 'Psychiatric Aspects of Civilian Disaster', *British Medical Journal*, 1 (1976), pp. 944-7; and J. Miller, *Aberfan — Disaster and its Aftermath* (Constable, 1974).

FIVE

Rites and Customs

Introduction

It can often be difficult to know what to say or do when a crisis occurs since our usual means of coping may seem inadequate. Therefore, all societies have developed forms of *ritual* which are built into their culture and provide acceptable ways for someone to behave in a disturbing situation.[1]

One very important group of ritual actions is that associated with life crises, which mark the passage from one social or religious status to another,[2] for example, the rituals relating to birth, marriage and death. One of the early major studies of these rituals was undertaken by Arnold van Gennep (1873-1957) who first employed the term *rites of passage*.[3] He saw these rites as a means whereby individuals might be eased, without undue social disruption, through the difficulties of transition from one social group to another. In this way Mary, whose husband had recently died, would make the change from being 'wife of John' to being 'widow of John'. Arnold van Gennep proposed three distinguishable and consecutive stages in this process:

Separation	or Pre-Liminal	(before the threshold)
Transition	or Liminal	(at the threshold)
Incorporation	or Post-Liminal	(past the threshold)

The person, or group, on whom the rite focuses is first symbolically separated from his or her old status, then undergoes adjustment to the new status during the period of transition. Finally there is incorporation into society with a new social status. The relevance of these three parts of a rite of passage will be discussed further in connection with the pastoral care of the dying and the bereaved. It is important to note that the rituals associated with the care of dying and the bereaved, and the disposal of the dead, do not replace the grief process. Rather the ritual is offered as a helpful structure or framework. If a ritual, or rite of passage, is to be relevant and aid the normal process of grief then it should meet needs at three levels:

The Psychological Level	—	by giving a framework for the full expression of feeling (grief) and to reduce anxiety.
The Theological or Philosophical Level	—	by which one seeks to make some sense and meaning out of what is experienced, in relation to the goal one is aiming for.
The Sociological Level	—	through sharing the experience with others and being re-accepted into society with a new status.

We shall consider the place of ritual in the grief process under two broad headings:

A.   Prior to the death
B.   Following the death

The Place of Ritual Prior to the Death

Making the relationship

Ideally our ministry to the dying person will have commenced long before the closing stages of life are reached so that we do not come as a complete stranger. This is equally true whether we are ministering to the person at home or in hospital. Sometimes we are called to a family or an individual in an emergency and there may be little time to build a relationship. Here one has to respond sensitively to the needs of the time and, if you do not know the family, remember they may see the minister as the forerunner of the undertaker!

Our previous knowledge and relationship with the dying person can influence the way in which we minister to them at the close of their life. To represent mortality is not always oppressive or frightening. Some of the people visited are very aware of what is happening to them and look to the clergy as people who are not afraid to talk of death. Ministers are also seen as people able to offer comfort and the reassurance of God's love as well as enabling people to 'die well'. This help may be offered through a relationship and through the use of familiar ritual and liturgical forms. Not everyone is familiar with a sacramental ministry and so there is a need for flexibility in the forms of worship used. There may also be people who wish to see a minister but who have had little or no contact with 'the church' for very many years, but still feel anxious about what is happening to them. They often do not know what they wish the clergy to do but they hope that the minister will be able to sort it all out. It is as if, like 'instant coffee', there is an expectation that the minister can provide 'instant faith'. Much teaching may be necessary with both the family and the sick person if unreal expectations are to be avoided.

In that we must all grieve our own grief so we must do our own dying, and face the possibility and reality of our own mortality, and others should enable us to do this in our own way. A very fundamental source of anxiety for many is what will happen to those left behind and what will the process of dying be like. Sometimes a dying person will ask to be *helped* to die. The work done in hospices and elsewhere shows clearly that such requests arise when a person's pain is not being properly controlled or when people are not listening or responding appropriately. The request for 'mercy killing' is frequently a challenge to care and an expression of unmet needs.[4]

Sometimes the anxieties of the family and their reluctance to face the reality of impending death will create obstacles for the clergy. A wife may stay in the room all the time and give little or no opportunity for the minister, or dying person, to talk about what is happening and what the person feels. It is sometimes easier to talk to the patient privately in the hospital than it is in the home if the relatives are not accepting of the patient's need to talk to a minister alone. This also applies to the relative as well as the dying person. The clergy may need to listen to simultaneously different needs. Because of their differing needs the relatives may 'protect' the patient from the minister because *they* cannot cope.

It is difficult to give set sayings for people to use in order to establish a more open relationship. One has to respond sensitively to what is happening and pick up what is conveyed in a look, a squeeze of the hand, a closed fist or eyes filling with tears. One has to listen to what is not said. To use a set opening sentence will usually guarantee that it will go wrong! If the person is anxious and upset one can sometimes ask, 'What did the hospital, or the doctor, have to say?' and then perhaps, 'What do you make of it all? How do you feel about that?' In some instances it may seem right to say, 'You seem upset today, are you in pain or are you feeling frightened?' These approaches allow the person to open up about their feelings and reactions to what is happening. If they do not wish to share their feelings, an open-ended approach allows the person to say, 'No, I'm fine,' and change the subject. We should avoid statements which corner the person or give them no let out.

The person who is dying grieves for the *impending* loss of their own life, in proportion to their awareness of what is happening. Therefore, we must expect to see and share in many of the normal grief reactions, already described, experienced by the dying person and the family. Death is not a single event but a process by which various functions of the body 'go to sleep'. Even after death has been certified, for example, the nails and hair continue to grow. The dying process, therefore, is one of gradually letting go. For this reason many dying people sleep a great deal towards the end of their life and so withdraw from contact and communication with their family and others around them. Whilst this is natural, relatives may not always understand it and try to rouse the person and engage them in conversation. This is another reason for the minister being involved earlier on in the illness so that relationships have been built, discussions concluded and he is now free to come and simply *be* with the person. It is often very difficult to just sit and *be* with someone, for we may long to *do* something. There can, however, be nothing more irritating for the dying than overbusy people who cannot keep quiet and hold your hand, but must keep 'plumping up' the pillows every few minutes and demanding to know if you are all right.

An important part of pastoral care is to learn the art of *being still* and *being with* people. Any ministry that we perform should, therefore, be in tune with the patient's condition at the time of our visit.

Simply being with the dying: hours together saying nothing: this is an ability which I dare say clergy should develop more than they possess it: the ability to sit with someone, saying or doing nothing. Not just sitting looking vaguely and vacantly about, just knowing that 'if I sit for half-an-hour I will have done my job': and not sitting with a sort of pious look—'I am praying next to my patient': and not talking in a pious or impious way . . . this ability, just to sit and go deep, so deep in sympathy, in compassion, is showing that you do not need these discourses, that your presence speaks: that if there is a need, you can put a hand on the person and it will mean more than whatever you can say.[5]

What are our pastoral aims to be?

There are four basic pastoral functions which can be identified in the pastoral relationship.

To reconcile: With the dying and the bereaved this function is very important and the need for reconciliation shows itself time and time again. People need help to re-establish broken relationships between man and God, between man and man, and frequently they need to be reconciled with themselves and assured of forgiveness.

To sustain: The dying person requires supporting and sustaining if he or she is to endure and transcend what is happening to mind and body. Here the ministry of word and sacrament can be especially important.

To guide: Many people look to the clergy at such times to guide them both in what to do and also in their understanding of the nature of God, the person of Jesus Christ, and the Christian understanding of Life after death.

*To enable
growth*:

If the individual is to grow and attain true health/wholeness/salvation then the minister needs time. When time is not available, reconciliation should become the focus, coupled with the understanding that this may enable growth to be achieved through dying and death.

It is interesting to note that, although different terminology is used, these same basic pastoral aims are reflected in the *Book of Common Prayer* order for the Visitation of the Sick. There the priest is directed to establish with the patient:

1. Penitence — sorrow for wrong-doing;
2. Charity — by restoring relationships, making a will, settling debts;
3. Increase of the sick person's faith.

These pastoral aims will best be achieved in the context of a sensitive, loving relationship so that the dying person comes to believe in God's loving acceptance as a result of our loving acceptance of them. It is envisaged that this relationship will extend to include those others involved in the care of the dying person. If the person is dying in hospital then there should also be good liaison between the parish priest/minister and the hospital chaplain.

Bible reading and prayer with the dying

Out of our relationship with the dying may come the request to hear a favourite passage of Scripture. It is helpful to check whether the person has a particular version in mind because the Twenty-third psalm in an unfamiliar version may either stimulate further thought or greatly irritate. Our aim is to minister to the other person's needs not our own!

Various authors have selected suitable passages of varying lengths which might be used with the dying, and the Bible Societies produce selections of attractive leaflets which can be left with people to use after your visit is over.[6] Because very ill people find it hard to concentrate the passages should be short and preferably familiar. However, we must avoid the temptation to use such readings as a means of avoiding dialogue or as a quick-exit line. 'Well, Mr Smith, I'm sorry I cannot stay longer but do remember — underneath are the everlasting arms.'

Because of drowsiness or unconsciousness it may be difficult to communicate *verbally* with the patient. The drowsiness may be drug-induced and by asking the times of medication one can sometimes arrange to visit during a more wakeful moment. If the person is unconscious one should still direct one's attention *to* the person and not *over* the person to the relatives. One can never be sure to what extent a seemingly unconscious person can still hear. Therefore, one should seek to pray *with* and not over the patient. For the same reason, one should be careful over what is said in the presence of the dying, even if they seem to be asleep. To pray 'We *commend* your servant, Alice . . .' may convey the meaning of 'Go forth upon thy journey . . .' and cause alarm and not comfort because the meaning was not clear. One day one of the authors was asked to see an elderly lady who was dying. After a long conversation he prayed with her and then said that he would commend her to God and bless her. As he said, 'Into your hands, O Lord, we commend your servant, Sarah . . .', she quickly stopped him and said, 'No! Not yet, Vicar, I'm not ready to go'. On another occasion the chaplain saw a man the night before he died. He said, on leaving, 'I'll see you sooner or later'. The man replied, 'Later rather than sooner, I hope'.

Flexibility in the prayers we use, and the way in which we pray, is also very important. A very tired and breathless person would find joining in a lot of prayers, or a long litany, too exhausting. If the person cannot join in the prayers it is helpful to suggest that they 'listen in their mind and say aloud the Amen'. Joining in or listening to the Lord's Prayer is very comforting, provided we pick the version they know. If concentration is poor people become very upset if they get lost and cannot remember the Lord's Prayer and so are often glad to say it with someone else. It is important that an affirmation of faith be included in our pastoral care of the dying. Once again, if the dying person is too ill to recite a creed one can use short questions to which the person may nod the head, say 'yes', or squeeze the hand. Sometimes we may need to make the affirmation on behalf of the person when we know this to accord with their belief.

The Sacraments

1. Baptism

During the course of one's ministry to the dying adult it may emerge that the person has never been baptized. If it accords with the wishes of the dying person then arrangements should be made to prepare the person at home, or in hospital.

> Janet was twenty-one years of age when she had her first baby. She had been receiving treatment for cancer of the face for six months prior to the birth of the baby and shortly after the child's birth moved into the terminal phase of her illness. The local vicar was contacted about the baptism of the baby and during his visit it emerged that Janet had never been baptized. After due preparation he arranged for a joint baptism in the living room of Janet and Bob's home, since Janet was too ill to leave the house. The service was truly a healing service. It not only spoke of incorporation into the Body of Christ, of initiation, but it also illustrated another aspect of a rite of passage in that it aided the grieving process for Janet, her family, and the local neighbours who were present.

In the hospital setting the chaplain may be contacted regarding the baptism of a seriously ill baby. The sacramental ministry in hospital is the chaplain's responsibility, though he will naturally co-operate with local clergy by informing them about emergency baptism or anointings performed. He may also contact local clergy regarding the follow-up of people with whom he has had special pastoral contact. Likewise, the hospital chaplain would expect referrals from local clergy of people with special needs and to be consulted if clergy wish to conduct some special ministry for patients at the bedside.

The usual criterion for mentioning baptism to parents in hospital is if the child is critically ill and may not recover. Also if the child is to undergo surgery or have tests which might pose a risk for the child, such as cardiac catheterization.

The decision should be that of the parents and not because of the anxiety of the others around. The parents, some of the staff involved and perhaps grandparents should be present if at all possible and one should guard against 'hole in the corner' ministry of the sacraments. Likewise instruction as to what one is doing is important to dispel thoughts of superstition or ideas of magic.

In baptizing critically ill children, or dying adults, one is not saying that to die unbaptized is to be rejected by God. One is performing in emergency the rite that the individual or family would still have wished to be performed were circumstances different. In emergency, of course, any lay person may perform the baptism and nurses are usually taught how to perform Trinitarian baptism, and to inform the chaplain subsequently. A certificate should be issued and entry made in the baptism register. If the child, or adult, lives then arrangements should be made subsequently for that person to be 'received into church'.

Where a dying adult has requested baptism it may also be appropriate for the hospital chaplain to contact the bishop and arrange for him to visit the patient to administer the rite of confirmation at the same time. Clearly the parish priest or minister would make the same arrangements with the bishop if the person was dying at home. Once again, hospital staff should be informed about the arrangements if the patient is in hospital. Quite often the hospital catering officer will arrange for a cake if due notice is given!

2. Sacrament of Forgiveness

If one of our pastoral functions is to assist reconciliation then it is important that the dying person should be instructed to examine his life and identify those areas where there is estrangement and pain. Some people will react strongly to the use of the word 'confession', whilst others will request the sacrament themselves. Those who dislike the term 'confession', will still often seek forgiveness and absolution, but may express this as a desire to 'put things right'.

It is helpful to invite the person to consider the state of their relationship with God, other people and themselves. One may then be able to help them to acknowledge areas where things are wrong, to express contrition and seek forgiveness. Because privacy is not always easy to obtain in a hospital ward it helps to sit close to the patient's head. Those who are used to administering Holy Communion in a hospital ward will know the sudden lull in the ward's conversation following the words 'I confess . . .' from behind a curtain! By sitting close one can often speak quietly, even to the partially deaf, without others overhearing.

Irrespective of churchmanship the movement towards reconciliation is an important part of achieving a peaceful death. In our earlier discussion of *rites of passage* we recognized three stages:

1. Separation;
2. Transition;
3. Reincorporation.

The sacrament of forgiveness is an important part of this process for it enables the dying person to let go of some of the ties with this life. It also resolves some of the anxieties about leaving this life in order to 'go to be with God'. This part of our pastoral ministry therefore greatly assists the dying person's growth in life.

3. Sacrament of Holy Communion
The Viaticum (the provision for the journey) is the term used for the last receiving of Holy Communion by a dying person. It is right that those who have been used to receiving Holy Communion in life should be given the opportunity to receive it at the time of their death. In the church of England, Canon B 15a allows for 'any baptised person in immediate danger of death' to receive Communion. Within the Roman Catholic Church 'those in danger of death from any cause are obliged to receive Communion'. This may either be given on its own or, if time allows, together with the sacraments of penance and anointing.[7]

The form of service used and the manner in which communion is administered will vary according to the condition of the patient. Sometimes members of the family can be present and can join in the service and thus receive the sacrament with the patient. The rule of fasting is, of course, relaxed. It is usual to shorten the service and to use previously consecrated bread and wine. It is often easier to carry the consecrated bread and wine in a double pyx than to use a chalice. At the time of the administration one can intinct a small portion of the host/wafer with the wine and place it into the patient's mouth. A sip of water afterwards can help the person to swallow. Alternatively a fragment of bread can be put into some of the wine on a spoon. If the person is unable to swallow or receive anything by mouth the person should be assured that all the benefits of communion are received.

On occasion it may be appropriate to consecrate the bread and wine in the presence of the dying person and family, but frequently the service has to be kept short. Where possible one should at least include an act of faith, an act of penitence, the Lord's Prayer, the administration of the consecrated bread and wine, and the blessing and commendatory prayers.

The Viaticum is thus seen as a very important rite of passage in that it is received by the dying person as a means of grace and strength to assist him or her in the transition from this life to a fuller experience of Christ's risen life.

4. Sacrament of Anointing or Unction

In recent years there has been a very necessary and right move to re-establish the practice of anointing as a normal part of the Church's ministry of healing. This has been aided by the move within the Roman Catholic church to talk of the 'Sacrament of the Sick' rather than 'Last Rites'. Because of the special nature of this sacrament it should be reserved for crisis situations in serious illness. Clearly the approach of death is *one* such crisis, but not the only one for which unction is appropriate.

If the person is to be anointed in hospital there should be close liaison between the hospital chaplain and the person's own minister, who may wish to be present or administer the anointing. Likewise the medical and nursing staff should be informed about the anointing and the family should be present if possible. The medical and nursing staff often appreciate the opportunity to share in the service.

The anointing may be administered following an act of penitence and before receiving the final Holy Communion, or may be performed separately. The oil used should be pure olive oil consecrated by the bishop of the diocese or by the minister himself in accordance with a recognized form of service.[8] At the time of anointing the minister dips his thumb into the oil and makes the sign of the cross on the forehead of the dying person. Sometimes the hands of the person are anointed also. There should be a piece of clean cotton wool available for cleansing the patient's forehead and the minister's thumb after the anointing. The wool should later be burnt. One form of wording for the anointing is:

> N, in the name of the Lord Jesus, I anoint you with oil. May our Heavenly Father grant you the inward anointing of his Holy Spirit of strength, and joy and peace. Amen.

If the dying person is unconscious and unable to receive Holy Communion it may still be appropriate to anoint him or her. We can never be sure how much an unconscious person can perceive and be aware of. On one occasion a seemingly unconscious patient made the sign of the cross twice during the administration of the laying on of hands and anointing, to the astonishment of all present.[9]

In many cases it may be most natural to include the laying on of hands at the same time as anointing the dying person. This may either take place immediately prior to the anointing or as part of the blessing at the end of the service.

If the dying person is a child who has been baptized, but not confirmed, within the Church of England Canon B 15a would allow for the child to receive Holy Communion and/or to receive anointing and the laying on of hands. Whether the dying person is an adult or a child it is important that time is spent preparing the family, the patient and others involved, concerning the meaning of what we are doing. The directness of a child and the depth of spirituality that one can experience with children make this part of our ministry both challenging and rewarding. It is only preparation which can avoid the danger of the sacraments being associated with magic and superstition. Such occasions can be important pastoral opportunities for teaching people about the Church's ministry of healing. It can also enable us to help people to appreciate that death can sometimes be part of the healing process.

5. Death-bed marriages
When someone becomes aware that they are approaching

death they may express a wish to be married before they die. Unfortunately novels and films have given the impression that if you break your leg on the way to your wedding you can get married in hospital instead. However, it is not as easy as that! Under the Marriage (Registrar General's Licence) Act 1970 there are specific arrangements for people who are terminally ill and who wish to marry. These arrangements are in addition to those which enable the Archbishop of Canterbury to grant a special licence for such a marriage to be solemnized according to the rites of the Anglican church.[10] If such a marriage is undertaken it is advisable that the sick person make a will. This should preferably be drawn up by a solicitor, but if this is not possible clergy and staff involved in the care of the patient should exercise caution before agreeing to witness such a will or codicil to an existing will. This is especially important if they are to be beneficiaries, or their church, or their employing authority — such as hospital, nursing home or hospice.

Commendatory prayers

At the time of the death or shortly before, it is appropriate to pray with or for the dying person and to commend them into God's loving care. There are usually at least two aspects to commendatory prayers:

1. Expressing confidence in Christ and his saving work;
2. Commending the dying to God's mercy and love.

Whilst the focus of such prayers is the dying person, the prayers may also have the effect of giving comfort and reassurance to the relatives concerning the victory of Christ over death.

Short texts or biblical readings may be used, or a litany may be said by those present. This can enable the family to have an active share in helping the dying person to 'die well'. It is interesting that most of the major world religions read certain passages of their sacred writings to the dying so that they may be a source of inspiration in their last hours. Prayers may also be made that the person shall safely pass, through death, from this life to whatever life is envisaged as being beyond death.[11]

Two forms of commendatory prayer within the Christian tradition are:

Heavenly Father, into whose hands your Son Jesus Christ commended his spirit at his last hour: into those same hands we now commend your servant . . . that death may be for *him* the gate to life and to eternal fellowship with you; through . . .

Go forth upon your journey from this world, O Christian soul, in the name of God the Father almighty who created you. Amen.

In the name of Jesus Christ who suffered for you. Amen.

In the name of the Holy Spirit who strengthens you. Amen.

In communion with the blessed Saints, and aided by Angels and Archangels, and all the armies of the heavenly host. Amen.

May your portion this day be in peace, and your dwelling in the heavenly Jerusalem. Amen.

At the Time of Death

As a person approaches death the level of unconsciousness deepens and the pattern of breathing alters. Because of moisture in the chest there may be a rattling sound which can alarm people. The breathing may also stop momentarily and then suddenly start again. Eventually a moment is reached when the muscles relax and the last breath escapes from the body. The heart stops and the person becomes very pale and gradually colder. There may be some slight muscular movement after death and this can lead people mistakenly to think that death has not yet occurred. In a hospital a nurse will usually examine the person and then call a doctor who will verify death.

If the person has died at home the family should remove excess bedding, leaving just one pillow, and lay the person straight. The mouth may be held closed by placing a suitable object under the chin, a pillow or book, and the eyelids closed. Heating should be turned off in the room and the doctor informed. He will come to verify death and to issue the death certificate. If the family have contact with a minister they should contact him and then the funeral director. If they have no contact with the church they should contact the funeral director who will help them make the necessary arrangements and remove the body from the home if that is their wish.

Washing the body is often undertaken by the funeral director, because nowadays not many communities have an official 'layer out'. The task of washing the body and laying out was often performed by a woman or group in the community who could be contacted by the family. This has traditionally been a task carried out by women as instanced by the women who came to the tomb on the first Easter morning to anoint the body of Jesus (Luke 23. 55-6). This preparation is often seen as a sort of last service and act of love for the deceased and a member of the family may wish to assist when this is performed at the home, or in hospital. The laying out is often concluded with prayer. Some religious groups have special prayers and rites for this washing and only certain people are allowed to perform the ritual. In the Muslim and Jewish communities those not of the faith should not wash the body of a deceased person since a non-believer could defile the dead person. For this reason an orthodox Jewish family would employ a 'watcher' to stay with the body from the time of the death until the time of the burial. With a Muslim the head would be turned to the right shoulder so that he can be buried facing Mecca.[12]

When the person has been receiving life-supporting aid prior to death, the definition of death may seemingly be more difficult. However, the British guidelines for the establishment of what has been termed 'brain stem death' have moved us away from only defining death as cessation of heart beat. In spite of controversy the tests laid down,[13] *if properly performed*, should lead to a clear diagnosis of 'brain stem death'. This is especially important if the family are to be approached, at a very emotive time, with a request for the donation of organs for transplantation. We do not feel that it is usually the minister's role to make such requests himself, but to accompany the doctor who makes the request and to be available to comfort and support the family at this time. On occasions, however, the chaplain may be the most suitable person, as mentioned in the Code of Practice.[14]

In certain circumstances the doctor may not feel able to issue a death certificate and may need to report the death to the coroner. The coroner will then look into the facts of the case and issue the certificate when he is satisfied as to the cause of death. This procedure covers deaths certified as directly or indirectly due to violence. Deaths which are sudden, attended by suspicious circumstances, or whose cause is unknown, will also be referred to the coroner.

If the deceased is a stillborn child[15] the doctor will issue a Medical Certificate of Stillbirth, instead of a death certificate, which should be taken to the Registrar's Office within six weeks. A certificate of burial or cremation will then be issued to the parents as for any other person who has died. In these sad situations the birth and the death have to be registered. As one father said later, 'It was the non-event of the year!' Most hospitals make it possible for the parents of a baby who has been stillborn, or who has died in the first few hours of life, either to make the funeral arrangements themselves with a funeral director of their choice or to sign a form authorizing the hospital to arrange the baby's funeral. In the latter case it is still possible for the parents of the child to be informed of the date and time, and for them to attend if they wish.[16]

Viewing the body

If the family were not present at the time of the death they may wish to see the body. This can either be in the chapel or viewing room attached to the hospital mortuary[17] or at the funeral director's chapel of rest. Sometimes this may happen in the ward of the hospital, as in the case of a stillbirth, where the parents may wish to see and hold their dead baby. It can be more natural for the person to be viewed either in the hospital bed or their bed at home, rather than in the starkness of a mortuary chapel or viewing room. One cannot lay down policies that everyone, or no one, should view the deceased. The next of kin has the right to see the deceased but the timing and place of viewing must be by mutual arrangement. In the hospital nurses should ask relatives if they wish a chaplain to accompany them when they view the deceased. Many relatives say 'Yes' and wish for prayers at such a time. There should be no rush at such times and occasionally staff may hurry relatives because they themselves are finding it difficult to cope. Viewing the body can help many relatives who are denying the reality of the death and so can be important for their subsequent grief work. Whilst not everybody will wish to see the deceased the opportunity to do so should be given to them.

If the clergyman is accompanying relatives to view a body following a road-traffic accident or similar incident it is advisable for him, or someone else, to see the body first. This then enables them to prepare the next of kin for what they may see. This is important if there are facial injuries or other disfigurement.

Clergy are sometimes asked whether children should go to view the body of a dead relative. One cannot be dogmatic about this. It depends so much on the child and the circumstances of the death. If it is a peaceful death at home then, *if the child wishes,* it can best take place by the child accompanying an adult after the laying out has been completed. In this way the child can hold an adult's hand and see the deceased in bed in a more natural surrounding than in a coffin at the funeral director's, and in this way say their goodbyes. We cannot 'shield' a child from what has happened. Frequently a child who shares the distress of the family may be able to use the experience in later life. One has to balance the short-term distress against the long-term effects of mal-adaptation over what might be the next fifty years.

Request for a post-mortem examination

It is not easy to ask a family for permission to perform a post-mortem examination. Sometimes there is little choice because it is required by the coroner for medico-legal reasons. In fact in the Jewish and Muslim communities permission for autopsy will usually *only* be given when there are medico-legal reasons for it. In all other cases the next of kin has the right to say no to a post-mortem if they object to it. Some families find it very hard to distinguish between 'head' and 'heart' and so although they know the person is dead will withhold consent because 'he has suffered enough already and they are not going to cut him up any more'. On the other hand some relatives are willing to consent because they wish to know the exact cause

of death, or need to know if the condition of a child is an
inherited one (i.e. they consent in order to help the living).
The request is usually made to enable the medical staff to
learn more about the illness which led to the death or to teach
medical students.

If consent is given for a post-mortem it will not usually
delay things very much. Every care is taken to ensure that the
face of the dead person is not altered so that the person can
still be viewed subsequently. When contacting a funeral
director it is important to tell him whether or not there is to
be a post-mortem.

If the deceased had arranged in life for his body to be
donated to the medical school's department of anatomy the
medical practitioner at the hospital or at home should be
informed prior to the death if possible. This fact should
certainly be communicated before any post-mortem examination is carried out. It is important during life that people
who wish their bodies to be given for dissection make the
proper arrangements with the university department of
anatomy, inform their next of kin, and understand that
sometimes the cause of death or the removal of organs may
lead the department to have to decline the offer. This can
upset relatives if they have not realized the possibility of this
happening. We shall comment later on the funeral
arrangements in the circumstances.

The Place of Ritual Following the Death

THE FUNERAL and associated events

The funeral is an extremely important event since it can be
the culmination of a process of care for the dying and the
bereaved. The way we die is a reflection of the way we have
lived. Similarly, the manner in which we dispose of our dead
can be a reflection of our attitude towards death, and towards
the person who has died.

The family of a faithful parishioner of the Anglican or
Roman Catholic tradition who has died may express the wish
for his body to be received into church the night before the
funeral and for a requiem to be said. The actual funeral

service would then be held the next day in the church, followed by committal of the body at either graveside or crematorium. In this instance the entire ritual is being set in the context of the worshipping community and is expressive of the life and belief of the deceased and the bereaved.

A family who have little or no contact with any place of worship, and who find it hard to face death, may request a 'short service'. They may leave the funeral director to make arrangements with the 'duty man' for the service and will arrange to 'meet you at the crematorium for a simple service'.

In contrasting these two different types of funeral no judgement is being made about the sincerity of feeling amongst those attending the funerals. The contrast is more concerned with different beliefs and attitudes towards death leading to differing requests concerning funeral arrangements. Both of these families, however, will have need to do their own 'grief work' and whatever their beliefs the funeral ritual will either help or hinder that grief process.

We referred earlier to the work done by van Gennep and others on *rites of passage* and the importance of these rites to facilitate the transition from one status to another. The funeral service and the events surrounding it can be very significant for both the deceased and the mourners. If the ritual is to facilitate grief the family and the community must be involved in the three aspects of the rite of passage:

Separation — Transition — Incorporation.

These three aspects are not rigidly separated from each other, but are a convenient way of identifying what the rite can signify for the deceased and the bereaved.

Separation

When a death occurs there is inevitably separation which may be gradual or it may be a sudden wrenching apart. However it happens the bereaved and the deceased must separate from each other and 'let each other go'.

Separation for the deceased
An important aspect of terminal care is assisting the dying person towards a dignified and peaceful death. If the minister

has been involved with the dying person at this stage of his illness then his pastoral care will have enabled him to say something about separation as well as reducing the anxiety of the dying. Being separated from those you love in this life raises the question of 'letting go into what?' This is a question about which clergy do have something to say.

Whilst the commendatory prayers at the time of death have the prime intention of commending the dying to God's mercy and love, they can also act as a means of giving permission for the dying to die. It not infrequently happens that following anointing, prayer and commendation the dying person will visibly relax and begin to 'slip away'. It is as if they feel that permission has been granted to let go and, therefore, they can now 'go forth upon thy journey'.

Separation for the bereaved

The bereaved must allow the dying to die and, having died, to let them be dead. Hence the need to declare the deceased to be dead in any prayers or ritual at this time, since it can aid separation. This is especially true if there is no physical body to see and touch as may happen if the person is lost at sea, or the body is donated to anatomy. Just as in the wedding service the priest says, 'I pronounce you man and wife together,' so in the funeral service he must declare the deceased to be dead, by not being afraid to use the words 'dead' and 'died'. Because of the shock and denial in the early part of grief we may need to re-state the reality of death several times, either verbally or through such actions as seeing the body and thus saying 'goodbye'.

It can be quite normal, if somewhat disturbing, for the bereaved to believe they have seen or heard the deceased in and around the home. A sense of presence is quite common. However, this is quite different from deliberately setting out to make contact with the deceased through spiritualism. By trying to contact the dead in this way we are attempting to hold them back instead of letting them go. Sometimes it is because we feel guilty and wish forgiveness or understanding from the dead person. It may simply be that we are seeking reassurance that they are 'all right'. To a Christian to hold on to the deceased in this way shows a lack of trust in a loving God. Jesus said to Mary in the garden, 'Do not cling to me . . .'

(John 20.17) and in the same way we must resist the temptation to cling. Rather we must allow separation to occur so that the departed is freed to go to God.

In some communities it is still the custom to draw the curtains at the front of the house from the time of the death until the funeral is over. This signifies to others that there has been a death and that the next of kin has withdrawn from the community and their normal pattern of living. It is also the cue for others to call and make condolence visits and offer help. The bereaved thus become *separated* in order to become the focus of care from both the family and the community. The placing of the 'death notice' in the local paper can be another way of bringing home the reality of the death even though the next-of-kin may not wish to look at it immediately. Similarly, condolence cards and letters are appreciated. Whilst they may not be read properly until much later, they do signify the support and prayers of others.

With urbanization, rehousing and changes in the family structure there are now many people who may be very isolated and receive little help at such a time. It has been shown recently [18] that, in one sample of bereaved people, 37 per cent received no help with the funeral arrangements and had to cope with it all on their own. In some blocks of flats neighbours may not know that there has been a death until they see a hearse outside. Separation of the bereaved from the dead and from the obligations of their normal living pattern is a temporary state, but can serve to heighten loneliness if there is insufficient support for the bereaved.

Pre-funeral visits by the clergy
The prime 'funeral director' should be the minister where he is already involved with the family as their parish minister. In that he will have cared for them during several previous life crises he is the one they turn to for guidance and help during a crisis. They will look to him for leadership and support to enable them to say and do things that 'feel right'.

Clearly there needs to be a good relationship and liaison between clergy and funeral directors. With those families who have no church connection the funeral director can fulfil an important caring role and may often pave the way for a visit by a minister whom they have not met. In many places

clergy and funeral directors work closely together and, as far
as possible, funerals are taken by the clergy who are likely to
have continuing pastoral contact with the bereaved. In spite
of the many jokes which connect clergy and funeral directors,
their mutual understanding of each other's role and support
for the bereaved can do much to enable growth from this
pastoral opportunity. Where a death has occurred in hospital
a referral to the appropriate minister by the chaplain (if he
has been involved) can give a lead-in for this first visit.

The pre-funeral visit to a family where one is known and
welcomed is quite different from that where you have no
previous pastoral contact. It is not usually a time for one-to-
one bereavement counselling. There is often much coming
and going, with relatives and friends in and out of the room,
and the next-of-kin perhaps shocked and numb. To the family
the main purpose for the visit is seen to be the necessity of
arranging the funeral.

There will be discussion of hymns, Bible reading, flowers,
burial or cremation, disposal of ashes, prayers at the house,
and the meaning and form of service to be used. If the dead
person has been brought back to the house this may lead to
prayer with the bereaved in the presence of the deceased.

Following the death of a three-year-old child in a traffic
accident the minister found, when making a pre-funeral
visit, that the front room had been cleared of all furniture.
In the centre of the room was the little coffin, surrounded
by toys and people were taken in to say 'goodbye' to the
child. The minister was also invited to 'see Anne' and thus
given the opportunity to talk about the deceased, the reality
of the death and to pray with the family by the coffin.

To pray or not to pray is a common question. If you ask the
family they often say 'yes' because they feel they should. A
prayer should not be a means of wrapping it all up, silencing
the family, or protecting the minister! There needs to be a
spirit of openness which echoes and offers up to the love of
God what has been shared in the visit — the positive and the
negative, the rage and doubt, submission and bewilderment.

Whilst there needs to be some discussion, there also needs
to be time to listen to what is happening within the family. A

home visit can enable one to build up a picture of the various and different reactions of family members, to assess where they are in their grief, and to gain information about the deceased. Various members of the family may be at different points in their grief which, coupled with previous rivalries, can lead to friction. Two sons may be competing to sort out mum's finances or it may be that the family is good at sorting out practical difficulties but not at coping with emotions. The extent to which the next of kin will be subsequently isolated when the family members return to their own homes may also be evident. It may also be possible to pick up whether the needs of younger children are being recognized, and whether they are being allowed to face reality.

As mentioned earlier, the family may feel angry with God for allowing the death to occur and to have seemingly brought about a separation which they did not want. While they need the minister to conduct the funeral they may resent his presence and intrusion into their territory, but tolerate his visit. On the other hand they may feel the need to impress on him what a 'good person' the deceased was and therefore worthy of a good funeral. This may be coupled with a readiness to accept whatever the minister suggests, even if it is not exactly what they feel, as if to placate him (or God) for previous non-attendance at church. Listening can help to uncover some of these ploys and to bring things back to a more realistic level. Discussion about the deceased and some of the good and bad experiences shared can be relevant and helpful on occasions if done sensitively. Discussion of the illness and the death may also help in putting the bereaved in touch with the *real* person from whom they have been separated.

The pre-funeral visit not only serves to prepare the family for the funeral, but can be important in aiding the separation because of the authority and status of the minister on such occasions. The visit also has the effect of preparing the 'agenda' for subsequent pastoral care at the funeral and later, and of communicating God's loving care at a time of pain and sorrow.

Transition

This is an in-between time while, for example, Mrs Jones *wife of . . .* becomes Mrs Jones *widow of . . . .* She may feel a stateless person until a new identity or social role has been formed and accepted. Likewise a couple whose child has died may feel the loss of the status of 'parent'.

Transition for the deceased

The transition for the deceased is related to the anxiety expressed by many bereaved people as to where the dead person has gone to. The concept of a journey is prevalent with many people and there can be great anxiety about 'hell, limbo and heaven', often disguised in jokes about 'Harry always being good with a shovel . . .' and strong feelings about cremation and the language used at the committal. Linked with this can be the anxiety that the dead in some way may be able to do harm. 'Never speak ill of the dead' has overtones of fear of reprisals as well as genuine respect for the departed. The obverse is sometimes seen with divorce where some may speak only bad of the divorced spouse. Public recognition of the death of the deceased is an important part of the transition, linked as it is with the public recognition of the length and value of the life of the individual. Such praise for the deceased may have the effect of assuaging guilt felt by the mourners, whilst also saying to God, 'Here is someone worthy of your attention'.

What we should be seeking to express at this time of transition is our faith and hope in God's love and grace, and not in what we have achieved in life. Eulogies, elaborate arrangements and sentiment can sometimes cloud this for us, whereas a genuine act of thanksgiving for the deceased and the family may reaffirm our dependence and trust in God.

An important part of liturgy, therefore, is to reaffirm the continuity in Christ of the living and the dead and the appropriateness of commending the departed to the mercy and love of God. It is for many the Eucharist and the Requiem which symbolize this most clearly. It may seem something of a paradox to the onlooker to see a practising Christian, at the funeral of a loved one, joyfully singing, 'Thine be the glory' with tears streaming down the face. However, there is a joy in knowing that the deceased is with God whilst at the same time grieving for the loss of their physical presence.

> I am sure that neither death, nor life, nor angels, nor principalities, nor things present, nor things to come, nor powers, nor height, nor depth, nor anything else in all creation, will be able to separate us from the love of God in Christ Jesus our Lord. [19]

Transition for the bereaved

> The interval between the decay of the old and the formation and the establishment of the new, constitutes a period of transition, which must always necessarily be one of uncertainty, confusion . . . [20]

For the bereaved the transition phase of the rite of passage is the time when the past is left behind and the future has not yet begun. It is the period between Good Friday and Easter Day. One's point of reference has gone and time seems to stand still as an endeavour is made to discover and accept a new identity and status. There can be much uncertainty and confusion as one looks to friends and family for help and support in adjusting to a new status as 'widow, orphan, single person'. The funeral ritual and associated events are a vital part of this because the funeral has the capability of encapsulating the full process of separation, transition and incorporation and thus enabling the bereaved to move forward in their grief. It does not do the grief work for them, but it can act as a catalyst. The extent to which the ritual achieves this aim of stimulating grief work is dependent upon several factors: what is done before the funeral service, the attendance and support of the family and friends, the individual character of the bereaved, and the level of actual involvement of those attending.

Family and friends

Several studies have been undertaken which have shown the importance of the funeral as a gathering of the kin and friends of the deceased. [21] There are regional differences in that the funeral and the gathering in the home afterwards have a much higher attendance in Scotland, Wales and northern England, than in the south of England. The findings indicate that there needed to be an obligatory occasion to make them visit.

The presence of the family and friends at the funeral service and at the house is comforting and also aids the acknowledgement of the new status. One researcher[22] suggests that 'the *bereaved* are comforted by the presence of *close kin* at that time and derive their sense of support from this and the general gathering, whereas it is the *other kin* who obtain a sense of solidarity and a reinforcement of kin relations by noticing in detail whom of their number attend'. The help given by the family and friends can serve to reassure the bereaved that they will be acceptable in their new role and status. A recent survey has summarized various ways in which family and friends helped the bereaved following a death.[23]

In addition to the help tabulated below 30 per cent of the surveyed group received financial help with the cost of the funeral. It is also significant that this same survey showed that most of the help given was practical rather than passive/emotional support, and that 37 per cent stated that they received no help at all. The presence and support of family and friends, both at the funeral and subsequently at the house, is something appreciated by the bereaved even if the motives for coming may be suspect in some instances. If the bereaved are to be aided in moving from old to new status they need to feel that other key people also acknowledge this change. The funeral service, therefore, is a key event in the total rite of passage.

The funeral service

> Meanwhile our eyes are fixed, not on the things that are seen, but on the things that are unseen: for what is seen passes away; what is unseen is eternal.[24]

During the course of the funeral rites our eyes are to be turned away from the physical remains towards the things 'that are unseen'. Away from who we are, and what we have done in life, to what God in his love has done for us through his Son, Jesus Christ. The service can direct us to the spiritual resources which can aid and encourage us to make the transition from the past to a future in which we must live the rest of our life.

Ways in which Family and Friends Helped the Bereaved
after the Death, Analysed by Status of the Bereaved[23]

		Total	Status of bereaved		
			Widow	Widower	Other
Base of percentages	weighted	758	312	125	321
	unweighted	764	313	123	328
Kinds of help specified:		%	%	%	%
Helping to arrange the funeral e.g. seeing the undertakers, contacting relatives, providing refreshments		57	57	58	56
Accompanying the bereaved when contacting officials or making funeral arrangements		35	32	41	35
Contacting 'officials' e.g. seeing the registrar or coroner, notifying insurance company or employer of deceased. sorting out deceased's affairs		33	43	25	27
Providing comfort or moral support e.g. staying with the bereaved, looking after the bereaved or his/her children		15	19	21	8
Sorting through and disposing of deceased's possessions		4	0	8	6
Giving advice to bereaved		3	3	2	9

The funeral is an event for all of us. In addition to speaking to the next of kin the funeral should also speak to those others present who may have experienced loss previously, or who may have been put in mind of possible future loss. Attending a funeral in whatever capacity can confront us with the fact that one day we shall die and all this will be happening for us. In that many people do not wish to be reminded of their own mortality they may not wish to be challenged in this way by the service and so may express the preference for a 'short simple service' at the crematorium where they may wish to be cushioned from facing the finality of physical separation by death.

If the funeral ritual is to be effective in facilitating the grief of the bereaved then those present must be actively involved. This may be by joining in with the responses, the saying of the psalms together, one of the group reading a lesson, singing a hymn, as well as the non-verbal ways of touching and holding each other and passing tissues. Apart from the clergy and the funeral directors most people are not familiar with the various funeral services of the different churches and so need careful direction so that they can be caught up in the ritual without becoming anxious about whether they should be standing, sitting or kneeling.

Apart from the planning of the service (preferably with the family prior to the funeral) and his own personal preparation, the minister has the key function of actually conducting it. He is invested with authority and looked to for leadership in seeing that the 'ritual is effective' and that 'Bert has a good send off'. It can be a daunting task to be faced with a varied group of distressed people, about whom one may know very little, and to try and unite them into a meaningful act of worship within the space of a few minutes.

> As pastors lead their congregations in prayer and worship and exhortation, they renew and re-symbolize their ability to be representative persons bearing the wisdom, resources, and authority of Christian faith. No other helping profession in our society possesses a ready way to exhibit ritually its representation of a distinct tradition of helping.[25]

The minister must endeavour to speak clearly and confidently, to look people in the eye, and to show that he is calmly in control of what happens. If we are to be able to proclaim the word and love of God in and through the service then we must be calm, confident and yet remain sensitive to what the people are feeling and may wish to express. David Shepherd has described this ability as *expressive leadership* by 'the man who can put into words the strong feelings of the group . . .'[26] The minister is, therefore, looked to as someone who is able to draw together the many emotions experienced by the people present and to offer them up as part of a true act of worship.

Many bereaved people are frightened by the intensity of their feelings, and the presence of other people whom they trust, coupled with a sensitive and calm leadership of the ritual, can enable them to feel safe about expressing feelings at the funeral. The funeral is something that mourners may dread in anticipation because of the finality of the physical separation which it rightly expresses. However, it is important to have a public recognition of the fact of death and to provide for the reverent disposal of the body. The Christian service also clearly proclaims God's love at the time of death and separation, commends the deceased to God's grace and care, and makes plain the eternal unity of Christian people (living and departed) within the risen Body of our Lord Jesus Christ. This is sometimes made difficult by the confusion between re-vivification and resurrection. Some people find it hard to distinguish between these two and feel that the Church has not always made it clear.[27]

When it is possible to set the funeral service in the context of the Holy Communion it becomes very clear that the prime task is to share in an act of worship rather than the ritual disposal of a body, important though that is. Sometimes this will take place as a requiem coinciding with the reception of the body into church the night before the actual funeral. On other occasions the funeral service and Eucharist will combine as the main church service prior to the committal of the body by burial or cremation. The eucharistic setting focuses our attention on Christ's sacrifice on the cross, our assurance of future resurrection, and reminds us clearly of the communion of saints. It also serves to emphasize that the funeral is not a private event and that others of the congregation may also be experiencing loss through the death of one of their members and may wish to be part of the communion and thanksgiving.

The sermon Whilst the words used and the framework of the liturgy are important to the effectiveness of the funeral rite, the sermon presents both a challenge and an opportunity to guide people towards a healthy resolution of their grief, and to refer to the transition that is taking place.

Historically there has been a reluctance to say too much about the deceased at the funeral and the Church of England Prayer Book makes no provision for a sermon. In the new Alternative Service Book the sermon is optional. This is not a time for an exposition of the psychology of grief. However, there is need to acknowledge the sense of loss and, where they are known to the minister, to reflect some of the emotions represented in those present. It is usually possible to include a note of thanksgiving and the pre-funeral visit will have given an opportunity to find out about the deceased, and the feelings that others had about him or her. Even when there is ambivalence in the various relationships it should be possible to find aspects of the person for which to give thanks, and to make some offering of the 'loose ends' of a person's life and the mourners connected with them.

What is said about the deceased, about the reality and certainty of death, and the feelings and reactions of the bereaved all needs to be set against the Christian teaching on death and resurrection and the belief in the ultimate union of all believers in Christ. Eulogy and sentimentality can detract from the basic Christian message.

The approach to the sermon will depend upon the circumstances surrounding the death, what we have gleaned about the family, and our own attitude towards death and the extent to which we personally have come to terms with it. It is hard to preach with confidence about something which causes us great anxiety. If this is the case it will be tempting to hide behind platitudes and thus be unable to convey conviction in what we are saying.

In addition we must learn the art of being aware and understanding what another is feeling—the anger, the doubts, the guilt, the fears for the future. In fact all the normal grief reactions described earlier. Because of the strength of some of these feelings the distressed mourner's attention may wander and only pick up the occasional sentence here and there. Therefore, one cannot develop involved theological arguments, but needs to use simple and straightforward statements. What is said and heard can go deep and stick for years in the minds of the mourners—for good and ill. As one lady said some years later, 'I don't remember much about what he said, but I could tell that he meant it'.

One difficulty, if we accept the thesis that the funeral can be an important rite of passage, is the tendency to reduce or to shorten the whole proceedings on the grounds that it is unnecessary suffering. There is also clearly a difference between the funeral of a faithful parishioner and the funeral for an unknown person conducted by the minister 'on duty' at the crematorium.

In the case of the funeral of someone we know nothing about prior to the arrival of the family at the burial chapel or crematorium, it is important to find some way of meeting the family before commencing the service proper. This can either be done in the chapel before starting the service, or by going out to the first car and introducing yourself to the chief mourners and making some personal contact. In this way you may at least find out what relationship they have to the deceased and you are expressing a concern to relate to them personally, rather than formally commencing the sentences and marching into the chapel. The funeral director can usually give you some information as to the manner of death: suicide, cot death, sudden coronary, or long-standing illness. Although there can sometimes be a desire not to hang about but to get on with the service, the five minutes or so that the above may take tells the family you wish it to be *their* service and that you appreciate it is their only one, even if it is your fifth as the 'duty man'.

It can occasionally happen that the 'duty minister' at the crematorium may be asked if he or she is willing to conduct a funeral service, for example for a Hindu or Sikh since there is no Hindu priest available. From the point of view of the family the Christian minister would be acceptable because he or she is to be revered as a 'holy person'. One can either refuse to take the service, or explain that as a Christian minister one would have to take a Christian service, or conduct the service and refer only to God. Time should be spent before the service commences to ensure that there is mutual respect for each other's beliefs and understanding about what is being said in the service.[28]

The funeral of an elderly person with no relatives or friends to mourn the loss can be a sad occasion. If the deceased person's estate cannot pay for a funeral this may lead to what is often described as a 'pauper or contract' funeral in a marginal grave, paid for by the Health Authority or the Local Authority. The funeral is usually early morning with the 'duty minister' and funeral director the only people present. Rather than a brief committal at the graveside, if we accept that each human being is special in the sight of God, then

there should be a decent funeral service to mark the end of
that life. If the person has died in hospital and has been a
long-stay patient the hospital chaplain can enquire whether
some of the staff or fellow patients may wish to attend. One
of the authors previously worked at a hospital where the
fellow residents in a unit for the mentally handicapped would
go by mini-bus to attend the funeral of one of their 'unit
family'. In spite of their handicap they too had grief to
express.

What if there is no body? We mentioned earlier that it is
important to have a public recognition of the fact of death
and this is especially important when there is no body to
grieve over. The deceased may have been 'lost at sea' or have
died in an explosion, or in the case of an early miscarriage or
abortion there may be no body to bury, but still a death to
grieve for.

It may be that the body has been donated to the university
for the purposes of anatomy. If this happens one condition is
that the remains be decently disposed of, with an appropriate
service, in accordance with the expressed wishes of the
deceased. This usually takes place about two years later and
the relatives can say whether they wish to be notified and to
attend at the committal.

In all cases where there is no body to dispose of it is
advisable that there should be some ritual to mark personally
and socially what has happened. A memorial service or a
requiem is often the right way to proclaim publicly the fact of
the death and to enable separation and transition to take
place. Failure to do something at this time may leave the
bereaved very unsure and anxious about how and where to
express what they are feeling. Grief may then be postponed
and this can be the prelude for abnormal grieving patterns
subsequently. If the bereaved is a patient in hospital at the
time of the funeral it can be beneficial if the hospital chaplain
visits to see whether the patient would like prayers, a service,
or simply some company at the time of the funeral.

In bereavement there is not only an external social change
of status, but also an internal change which is initiated by the
grief process. In the funeral ritual the next of kin is assured
that he or she will live on without the deceased. The

separation is represented as a completed one and the survivors are encouraged to make the transition to their new social identity leading to incorporation back into the community.

Reincorporation

This third part of the rite of passage aids the re-entry into the community of those who have been branded or stigmatized by death.[29] In that the funeral encapsulates the entire rite of passage, in miniature, then such re-entry can be symbolized by the return to the house of family and friends following the funeral. People usually return to the house for an act of group sharing. It is a time for offering support to the next of kin, for reminiscence, renewing old acquaintances and perhaps for settling old scores. Traditionally there is a meal and drinks. A great deal of emotion is expressed as laughter or tears, and on occasions it can lead to a riotous party. Such gatherings are more common in the north of Britain than in the south.

> The wake itself signifies a return to chaos, a release from the restraints of normal 'good behaviour' and propriety, a real cultural disintegration, analogous to the dissolution of the deceased's earthly identity and authority. The final requiem and burial are thus islanded in time, and attain a kind of post-cathartic solemnity, the deliberation of grief is acknowledged and accepted, the calm of all passion spent. Such post-liminal rites act as monuments to whatever has gone before; not only the death of people or animals, but of institutions, epochs, stages of growth, even attitudes of mind. They are real 'rites of passage'.[30]

In some parts of the country it is also the practice for the family to attend their local church on the Sunday following the funeral and for the deceased and family to be referred to during the course of the service. This helps to symbolize the on-going concern for the bereaved by the local Christian congregation.

Active support for the bereaved may not continue for very long. The family may need to return home to various parts of the country, the neighbours need to return to the needs of work and their own families. People also get tired of hearing what 'a marvellous husband Harry was'. Sometimes it is the bereaved who withdraw from the community. In the early days following the death the next of kin may be very open about their personal life and financial affairs with other people. Later they may wish that they had not talked so freely with some people and so may withdraw and, in effect, say to others 'keep out'. This often causes hurt and if other people do not understand they stop visiting and make such comments as, 'Fancy not letting me in, after all I've done for her'.

If the bereaved go away to stay with relatives immediately after the funeral this can delay or complicate *incorporation.* By going away at this stage the community does not have the easy opportunity to visit. When the bereaved returns home weeks later the community has returned to its normal activities and the opportunity and stimulus has been lost for visiting and support. This can lead to a heightening of the isolation that the bereaved will experience anyway.

Full incorporation of the bereaved back into the community is parallel to the final phase of grief which we described earlier as *'resolution'.*[31] We are, therefore, thinking in terms of a period of time nearer to eighteen months than the two or three months that people usually allow. Attempts to hurry the grief process are often an expression of *our* anxiety and embarrassment in the face of grief. A difficulty that faces many people in our own society is the lack of a structure within which to do their grief work, and which would mark off the end of grief.

Within the Jewish community, for example, there is a clear structure which is designed to aid the expression of grief: After the burial the community turns its attention to the next of kin, and on the return from the cemetery a meal will have been prepared as an expression of their care and the period of consolation begins. First there are three days for deep grief. The remainder of the first seven days *(Shiva)* of mourning are for condolence calls to be made, the visitor's main role being to listen not to talk, and to prepare food for the mourner. The remainder of this initial period of thirty days is for gradual adjustment known as *Shaloshim,* during which the mourner may return to work but lives a restricted life. The full period of mourning for a parent is one year from the date of the death, and so the remaining eleven months are for remembrance and healing until *Jahrzeit* (anniversary).[32] A tombstone may be erected and consecrated during this period and at *Jahrzeit* the *Kaddish* is recited in the synagogue and a memorial candle is lit. At the end of the year it is expected that the mourner will be well integrated back into the life of the community. Not all members of the community will adhere equally strictly to this pattern however.

In the absence of such a structure the bereaved look to various key people in the community for guidance as to whether certain actions are deemed acceptable or unacceptable and when grief may be officially 'ended' in the sense that it is all right to socialize. A young widow who wishes to remarry may seek approval from the local community in case she is censured later for marrying 'before her first is cold in t' grave'. One key person is the minister and this serves to underline the importance of post-funeral visits.

The post-funeral visit

In a busy pastoral area, with many funerals, one may argue that there is little time for a minister to make all the post-funeral visits that he might like to make. However, because of the special role that he has in society, the minister as well as being the person who conducted the funeral is often the only person who can make an uninvited call on the bereaved. Perhaps one reason for not making such calls is related more to uncertainty about the purpose of such visits rather than lack of time. If we are unsure about what to say or do then it is not difficult to find reasons to postpone a visit.

Unlike the pre-funeral visit where there may be a clear agenda and lots of other people around, after the funeral the minister is more likely to find the bereaved on their own. By this time the person will be less shocked and many of the feelings of grief may be under the surface waiting for an opportunity to be expressed. Since many people like to put on a good face for the minister we may gain the impression that all is well and that there is no need to rush back. One of the prime purposes of this visit, and any subsequent calls, is to provide an opportunity for the expression of grief if the person wishes to. If the minister is prepared to listen in an accepting way the bereaved will sometimes feel that it is safe to express, for example, some of the ambivalent feelings about the deceased and about God.

Whilst exaggeration of grief feelings may be fairly obvious, one should also take note of stoicism which can be equally unhelpful. Some Christians feel that grief is inappropriate for them and that they should be happy that their loved one is with God. This may lead to their exhibiting stoical indifference in the face of death and reassuring the minister that they are 'content and happy'. Here the person is saying to the minister what he or she thinks he wants to hear, a sort of 'baptized stoicism'. This response to loss often leads to delay or postponement of grief until the person feels they have permission to grieve and that it is not exhibiting lack of faith in God.

If the minister can talk about how normal, though distressing, a thing grief is this can often give reassurance where the bereaved may secretly have felt very worried about their reactions. A reference to the way in which Jesus expressed grief when his friend Lazarus died [33] may also help the person to feel safe in expressing some of their feelings.

> We have not incurred any grievous sin by our tears. Not all weeping proceeds from unbelief or weakness. Natural grief is one thing, distrustful sadness is another . . .[34]

The bereaved may also find it difficult to pray and to realize the presence of Christ with them in their grief. This can be a time to assure them that others are praying for them in spite of their feeling that God is absent.

> Meanwhile, where is God? This is one of the most disquieting symptoms. When you are happy, so happy that you have no sense of needing Him, so happy that you are tempted to feel His claims upon you as an interruption, if you remember yourself and turn to Him with gratitude and praise, you will be—or so it feels—welcomed with open arms. But go to Him when your need is desperate, when all other help is vain, and what do you find? A door slammed in your face, and a sound of bolting and double bolting on the inside. After that silence . . .[35]

Another function of the post-funeral visit can be to aid the bereaved in freeing themselves from painful associations. For example, the widow whose husband was a member of the church choir may find she cannot face going to church for a while because she keeps seeing the gap where her husband used to be. The minister's visit to the home may help the widow to feel that until she is ready to go to church, then the church will come to her.

The church, of course, is more than the minister and many congregations may be able to share in the post-funeral visits. Some ministers keep a card-index file so that they can ensure that they make a visit near to the time of the anniversary. We do not wish to advocate 'professional neighbourliness', but if a Christian congregation is to be actively involved in such visiting they need to be prepared and supported.

The sort of preparation envisaged is that which should be a normal part of our ministry to the congregation, namely helping people to focus upon death in the context of the resurrection. At any one moment the congregation will contain people who are preparing to face *future* grief and people who are working through *past* grief. The main difficulty for many people, which makes visiting the bereaved difficult, is their own anxieties about death and dying.

The Christian congregation should be one group in society whose members are willing and able to share the pain of loss experienced by others. This should partly be because their faith and instruction enables them to overcome the fear of death, and partly because they have the backing of a supportive and prayerful group. Where such pastoral visits by the local congregation are feasible the visitor can refer appropriate people to the minister. They will also be expressing in a practical way that the church cares and thus be enabling the gradual re-incorporation of the bereaved back into the community.

There are other groups who can offer support in various ways to the bereaved: *The Society for Compassionate Friends* — which is for parents who have lost a child; *Cruse* — for widows and widowers and other members of the family; The *Stillbirth and Perinatal Death Association*.[36] These and other self-help groups are made up of people who have experienced similar types of loss, and have been able to complete their grief work in a healthy manner. These groups usually have professional advisers who can offer support, expert advice and training as required.

Post-funeral visits may not be easy but they offer great pastoral opportunities. However, one of the biggest sins that can be committed by the minister, or any other visitor to the bereaved, is that of promising to visit and then never making that visit. Nahum Tate recognized this temptation when he wrote:

> Take the bowsey short leave of your nymphs on the shore,
>   And silence their mourning
>   With vows of returning,
> Though never intending to visit them more.[37]

Headstones and memorials

Because of the difficulty of letting go, and the wish to have a tangible reminder of the deceased, a suitably inscribed headstone or plaque is usually erected on the grave or other suitable place. Some of our forebears erected very elaborate tombstones. It is difficult to know whether the size was in proportion to the real (or imagined) importance of the deceased, or to ensure that the deceased stayed where they were!

Many church authorities have clear instructions about headstones to discourage ostentation as well as to aid the upkeep of the churchyard. An alternative way for many people to commemorate and 'immortalize' the deceased is to give a gift in memory to the church or some other institution such as a research body connected with the cause of the person's death. Gifts to the church should be 'to the glory of God' first and in memory of the deceased second. Problems can sometimes occur if the bereaved give a gift without prior consultation. Refusal of an inappropriate gift is often seen as a slight against the deceased.

It is important that the mortal remains of a baptized Christian should be decently laid to rest and therefore the cremated remains should be interred and not scattered in some inappropriate place like a golf course or cricket pitch. The interment of ashes often occurs later with appropriate ritual and prayers in either a specially appointed churchyard or crematorium garden of remembrance. Care should be taken to manage the interment so as not to **cause distress** to relatives by ash blowing on them. Where possible the ashes should be interred in the casket.

Prayers for the dead

One of the purposes of ritual is to reduce anxiety, and the anxiety about what has happened to the deceased has influenced aspects of the religious ritual throughout the history of the Church.

In the early days of the Church this anxiety led to the practice of baptism of the dead. This practice later disappeared and gave way to prayers for the dead. St Augustine was then influential in shaping much of the thought on this topic when he stated that intercessory prayer could do more to increase God's mercy than any pompous funeral or huge commemorative stone which (while comforting the living) was of no avail to the dead. It was out of such intercessory prayer, together with Holy Communion at the graveside, that the Mass for the Dead grew. Coupled to this was the development of the doctrine of purgatory and the growth of the chantry system[38] with all the attendant abuses. The Reformation sought to change all this and, as a result, praying for the dead has been a controversial subject for many ever since.

Within the Church of England, the Doctrinal Commission sought to resolve the conflicts by producing, in 1970, a report entitled *Prayer and the Departed*.[39] This document, with the ensuing debate, was important in the formulation of the funeral service in the Alternative Service Book (ASB) of the Church of England.

Those who disagree with petition for the dead argue that such prayers are unnecessary for someone who is already 'in Christ' for he or she is already enjoying rest and peace in Christ. They would further argue that to pray for non-Christians is wrong because it is in this life that they should make their decision about Christ. Otherwise one could put off making one's decision until after death when either 'the light is turned out' or you know for sure that the gospel is true. Praying for the dead, it is further argued, undermines the Christian assurance of being in Christ since it implies that something may be lacking which needs fulfilling after death.

Those who support petition for the dead claim that if we believe in the communion of saints then we should continue to pray for those we love who have passed to a new mode of existence. Similarly there is no reason why we should not ask them to pray for us. If, instead of dying, they had gone to live in Manchester we would not hesitate to contact them and ask them to pray for some particular need. We would also pray for them as they commenced their new life in Manchester. In praying for the dead one is not asking God to change his mind about the person for, after all, he knows them better than we do. Rather we are expressing our faith and trust in God's loving mercy to 'grant that your servant may know the fulness of life which you have promised to those who love you'.[40] A further point made by those who support prayers for the dead is that if we are not undermining the doctrine of justification by faith when we pray for someone who is alive, why should we be implying a denial of that doctrine if we pray for them after death?

Whatever our personal doctrinal position regarding prayers for the dead, many of the relatives we meet following a death are looking for reassurance and an easing of their anxiety about what has happened to the person who has died. The commendation of the departed to the loving mercy of God, an act of thanksgiving for the life shared, the belief in the resurrection and the hope of meeting again, represent areas of agreement for many. This agreement is well expressed at the end of the funeral service of the Church of England:[41]

> May God in his infinite love and mercy bring the whole Church, living and departed in the Lord Jesus, to a joyful resurrection and the fulfilment of his eternal kingdom. Amen.

Before offering any prayer at the time of death, therefore, the minister needs to spend a little time picking up the feelings that are around in the family regarding both the deceased and God. This reflects what was said earlier that if a ritual is to be seen as relevant it must be in tune with needs at the psychological, theological and sociological levels.[42] This sensitive 'picking up of the atmosphere' will enable the clergyman to formulate a prayer or prayers which express the reality of what is being experienced. Therefore, rather than picking up a book to say what we always say on such occasions, we must try to find out what *they* wish to be said. Such prayer, therefore, will usually include an act of thanksgiving, a commendation of the dead person, a reaffirmation of the Christian assurance that we are united in Christ from whom nothing can separate us,[43] our hope for future resurrection, and a request that God will grant to those who mourn strength and courage to face the future.

The mixed feelings which take place in certain relationships may also be reflected in these prayers when it seems right to do so. Sometimes one has the impression that by the use of *'requiescat in pace'* the family are implying the wish that the dead stay where they are and do not return!

The Holy Communion and the Requiem represent a unique meeting point between God and man, between the living and the departed. For those who believe in the sacramental presence of Christ in the consecrated bread and wine, they can also feel very close to the faithful departed (who are in Christ) when they go forward to receive communion. It is for this reason that many find that apart from their normal regular attendance at Communion a special annual occasion, such as All Souls' Day on November 2nd, can be especially significant and reassuring regarding *incorporation* for the deceased.

Children and funerals

A child's attitude to death will be coloured by our own and if we are not able to face the fact of death they will find it difficult also. To tell the child that 'Mummy is in hospital', when in fact Mummy is dead, can lead to a multitude of problems later. The distrust of the adult by the child, the fear of hospitals and the idea that any separation might lead to death can all result from this avoidance. It does not help to shut a child out of the grief that a *whole* family shares since this does not give them an opportunity and structure within which to express their grief.

Some recent research has shown that certain groups of bereaved children are more likely to develop subsequent psychiatric disorders later in life than others. The children at most risk are those bereaved of a parent at 3-5 years, or in early adolescence.[44] In view of what has been said about the possible efficacy of ritual in the grief process, should a child attend a funeral of a close relative? One cannot be dogmatic and say that all should or should not attend a funeral since it depends on who has died, the age of the child, the attitudes of the family and the form of service to be used.

It is important, above all things, to try to find out what the *child* wishes to do and not to be overprotective. However, in encouraging the child to talk we must also beware of the temptation to rush the pace. It is difficult for a child to make a decision without knowing what they are likely *to see* and be involved in. Therefore we should try to explain the funeral service and what the coffin will be like. All of us have our own way of explaining things to our children and we often use our own language. One mother explained to her daughter that just as you have a special casket for precious jewellery, so a coffin is like a special casket to hold something very precious — the body of the person who has died.

Where the committal is to be preceded by a service in church it may be decided that the child attends the church service and then returns home with a member of the family while the others go to the graveside or crematorium. Some children may wish to attend the entire ceremony, whilst others may decide to go and stay with someone until it is all over. One ten-year-old who attended the funeral service in church of a close relative sobbed afterwards and then said, 'Oh, I'm glad I came'. Whatever is decided it seems important that the child should have a say in the decision and an opportunity to express his or her own feelings about what is happening. Then the child's choice should be accepted as right by the family, without judgemental comment.

> Children have a lot of life to live, so it is important to guide them in such a way that they develop wise and healthful attitudes toward their feelings, their lives, and their deaths.[45]

Conclusion

We have looked at ways in which ritual does not replace 'grief work' but can, if used effectively, enable the grief process to happen. In that people in a crisis usually benefit from having a structure within which they may safely express very powerful feelings, the desire to reduce ritual to a minimum is not something necessarily to be welcomed. If we dispense with ritual we may leave people with a further sense of loss in that, not only have they lost a person through death, but they have also lost a means of coping with that loss. A recent review of six bizarre cases[46] where the next of kin kept the dead person in their home and did not arrange for burial, highlights the way in which three of these situations arose because the surviving relative failed to initiate the appropriate ritual. Decline in ritual in our society is not the only factor leading to unusual expressions of grief, but it can be an important one.

We are not here advocating a return to the codification of death rituals as developed in Victorian times as instanced in 'Manners and Rules of Good Society' (*The Widow,* 1887):

> The regulation period for a widow's mourning is two years. Of this period crêpe is worn for one year and nine months. For the first twelve months the dress is entirely covered with crêpe. The remaining nine months it should be trimmed with crêpe heavily so for the first six months and considerably less the remaining three. During the last three months black without crêpe should be worn. After the two years half mourning is prescribed . . . [etc.]

What we wish to assert is that a sensitive and flexible approach to the needs of a particular family should lead to a more relevant and effective ritual which can aid the grieving process. Since an inappropriate and ill-prepared ritual may serve to block the grief process this places a large measure of responsibility on those who arrange the ritual, as well as those who participate in it.

Notes

1. P. W. Speck, *Loss and Grief in Medicine* (Baillière Tindall, 1978).
2. See Appendix C.
3. A. van Gennep, *The Rites of Passage* (Routledge, 1977).
4. R. Lamerton, *Care of the Dying* (Penguin, 1980).

5. Archbishop Anthony Bloom, a talk to hospital chaplains, quoted by N. Autton in *Care of the Dying* (SPCK, 1966), p. 86.
6. N. Autton, *Watch with the Sick* (SPCK, 1976).
7. See S. R. C. Eucharisticum Mysterium, No. 39: AAS 59 (1967) 562.
8. See literature of Guild of S. Raphael; Church in Wales, 'Services for the Sick', or 'A Pocket Ritual' (post-Vatican II) (Mayhew-McCrimmon) for suggested forms of service.
9. P. W. Speck, 'A Relative Nuisance' in *Religion and Medicine,* 3 (SCM, 1976), p. 37.
10. In the case of the Anglican rite the dying person or intended spouse should contact the hospital chaplain or parish priest. They will then make an application to the Registrar of the Court of Faculties at 1 The Sanctuary, London SW1.

    When the parties wish to be married by non-Anglican rites, or to have a civil ceremony, a personal application should be made by the intended spouse to the local superintendent registrar. The applicant will be required to produce 'a certificate of a registered medical practitioner showing that the person concerned is seriously ill and is not expected to recover and cannot be moved to a place at which in the normal way the intended marriage can be solemnized, and that THAT PERSON IS ABLE TO AND DOES UNDERSTAND THE NATURE AND PURPORT OF THE MARRIAGE CEREMONY'.
11. John Prickett (ed.), *Death* (Living Faiths series, Lutterworth, 1980).
12. P. W. Speck, *Loss and Grief in Medicine,* chapter 8.
13. *The Removal of Cadaveric Organs for Transplantation — A Code of Practice* (DHSS, 1979).
14. ibid.
15. That is, a foetus born dead after twenty-eight weeks gestation.
16. DHSS Circular DS 211/75 which comments on HM (72) 4.
17. Hospital chaplains should check the mortuary chapel/viewing room arrangements at their hospital, and the policies dictating how they are used. They should also ensure that these areas are adaptable for use by non-Christians.
18. P. J. Hennessy, *Families, Funerals and Finances* (Research Report No. 6, HMSO, 1980).
19. Romans 8.38-9 (RSV).
20. J. Calhoun, *A Disquisition on Government* (1850).
21. M. Young and P. Wilmott, *Family and Kinship in East London* (Routledge, 1957); J. B. Loudon, 'Kinship and Crisis in South Wales', *British Journal of Sociology,* 4 (1961); G. Gorer, *Death, Grief and Mourning in Contemporary Britain* (Darton, Longman and Todd, 1965).
22. R. Firth, J. Hubert and A. Forge, *Families and their Relatives: Kinship in a Middle Class Sector of London* (Routledge, 1970).
23. Hennessy, op. cit., p. 29, Table 2.10.
24. 2 Corinthians 4.18 (NEB).
25. W. A. Clebsch and C. R. Jaekle, *Pastoral Care in Historical Perspective* (Harper and Row, New York, 1967), p. 68.
26. D. Shepherd, *Built as a City* (Hodder and Stoughton, 1974), p. 287.

27. G. W. H. Lampe and D. H. McKinnon, *The Resurrection* (Mowbray, 1966).
28. For details of other funeral rites and key texts employed, see J. Prickett, *Death* (Lutterworth, 1980).
29. An individual who is seen as being socially 'abnormal' may be reacted to by others in a variety of ways ranging from rejection to over-hearty acceptance or plain embarrassment. Close contact with death can lead to social contamination (stigmatization) and therefore the need for some form of cleansing prior to reintegration into society. One example of this process is seen in the healing of the ten lepers who were sent to the priest to be *pronounced* clean in order to rejoin their family and community (Luke 17.14). For further discussion of 'stigma' see E. Goffman, *Stigma* (Penguin, 1968).
30. R. Grainger, *Language of the Rite* (Darton, Longman & Todd, 1974), p. 120.
31. See Table 1 on page 13.
32. For the death of a child, spouse, brother or sister the period of mourning is reduced to thirty days.
33. John, chapter 11.
34. St Ambrose, on the death of his brother.
35. C. S. Lewis, *A Grief Observed* (Faber, 1973), p. 9.
36. For the addresses of these and other helping groups, see Appendix A.
37. Nahum Tate, *Dido and Aeneas*, Act III.
38. The benefices maintained to say or sing Mass for the soul of the founder and his friends.
39. *Prayer and the Departed*, Report of the Archbishop's Commission (SPCK, 1971).
40. Alternative Service Book, funeral prayers, section 60.
41. ibid., section 13.
42. See p. 62.
43. Romans 8.39.
44. D. Black, 'The Bereaved Child', *Journal of Child Psychology and Psychiatry*, vol. xix (1978), pp. 287-92.
45. F. Jackson, *The Many Faces of Grief* (SCM, 1978), p. 85.
46. A Gardner and M. Pritchard, 'Mourning, Mummification and Living with the Dead', *British Journal of Psychiatry*, no. 130 (1977), pp. 23-8.

SIX

When Grief Goes Wrong

*Those who mourn may mimic madness
to the observer's eye.*[1]

Whilst a normal grief reaction may, in Freud's words, mimic
madness there are times when the grief process goes wrong
and does not progress naturally towards *resolution*. In these
instances, rather than mimicking madness it may actually
lead to psychiatric illness and the need for professional help.

There are various ways in which grief can 'go wrong' and
in this chapter we shall look at some of these ways so that
those who are involved pastorally may recognize when an
appropriate referral may be needed. Although atypical forms
of grief do differ in intensity and duration from the more
usual reactions to bereavement already described, they do
not differ in kind.

There are no symptoms that are peculiar to pathological grief
although it seems reasonable to view extreme expressions of
guilt, identification symptoms (hypochondriacal illness), and
delay in onset of grief of more than two weeks' duration, as
indicators that the reaction to bereavement may take a
pathological course.[2]

Delay is the most common abnormal reaction and the
postponement of grief may be a short one, or may be delayed
for many years. People who have been involved in a disaster
may delay expression of grief because of the need to care for
others. The delayed grief may then be expressed many
months, or years, later following a relatively minor loss. For
example, a young woman whose husband was killed in a car
crash delayed her grief because of her concern to care for her
young chidren. Ten months later she was washing up, after
the children had gone to school, and broke a glass which had
been part of a wedding present. This led to the expression of

a severe grief reaction with her smashing the rest of the glasses and screaming out her rage at the husband who had 'left her'. The situation was controlled by the next-door neighbour who rushed around to see what was happening and called the doctor, and stayed with the young widow.

If a woman suffers a bereavement during pregnancy she may interrupt or delay her mourning, because of her preoccupation with the new life within her. Lewis[3] has shown that this may lead to idealization of the child within her and the child may then be seen as a reincarnation of the dead person. An example of this tendency was given earlier[4] when we discussed the Jenkins family and the mother's feelings about the child she was carrying. Lewis advocates that a 'bereaved woman should be helped to mourn at the time of death and to keep alive the expectation of future mourning once her baby is thriving'.[5]

This advice may perhaps be extended to other instances where postponement of grief may be anticipated. A normal part of grief is a period of total pre-occupation with the deceased and thus, if there are other people 'competing' for that mental space, either the others will be neglected or the grief will be postponed. This, therefore, supports the importance of the funeral and the associated events as giving space and permission to the bereaved to opt out of any responsibility for others for a short while and express some of their feelings. It also emphasizes the importance of maximum involvement of the bereaved in the funeral arrangements and anything which can establish the reality of what has happened. It may well be that, following the funeral, they will then suppress the grief but the acknowledgement of the reality of the death should have taken place. It is also important that those who are caring for the bereaved give fresh opportunity for the continuation of mourning, once the factors necessitating delay become less urgent. Failure to do this may mean that the person never restarts their grief work and this may lead to subsequent psychiatric illness in later life. If several people are involved with the family there may need to be some consultation between them to decide who is to be the 'key worker' to avoid confusion.

Denial. Because of the pain of separation some people may seek to avoid it by denying reality. To alleviate the constant

awareness of the loss the mourner who is expressing excessive
separation anxiety may turn to drugs or alcohol, with the
attendant danger of addiction or overdose. A glass of whisky
at night may help some people to sleep better, but having
your teenage child put you to bed because you are in a
drunken stupor is quite different. Similarly at certain times in
the bereavement the person may need drug medication to
calm down or to help them sleep. The selective and short-
term use of sedation is clearly right in some instances but can
in itself delay the grief process. Hence one should not resort
to drugs automatically because of psychological pain because
one may still have that pain to work through at a later date. It
is the abuse of alcohol or drugs that causes concern rather
than the controlled use of them.

There are various other factors which may lead to delay or
denial. It may happen because of a previous psychiatric
illness such as a personality disorder. It may be because there
is no body to see and to bury and so the reality of the death is
difficult to accept. It may be because the death itself is seen
as socially unacceptable, such as the suicide by a drug addict
which led her father to say, 'I never had a daughter,' and thus
there was no one to mourn for. The death of a divorced
spouse may lead to a similar reaction in that the divorced
partner may feel unable to attend the funeral. Feelings of
ambivalence or distress at the death of a former marriage
partner may reawaken feelings concerning the divorce. These
feelings may all be suppressed if one's current marriage
partner, or other members of society, deem such grief
inappropriate.

Prolongation of grief can be another common problem in
that any aspect of the normal grief process may persist for an
excessively long time resulting in the person becoming 'stuck'
in one particular part. For example, denial, anger, guilt or
idealization may persist for many years, and loneliness and
social isolation often heighten these problems. If a person has
become 'stuck' it can sometimes help if someone can spend
time taking them back over the events leading up to the
death, the death itself, the funeral and the feelings experienced
at that time.[6] For some people this may be sufficient to get
their grieving under way again. If not then a referral to
professional help may be necessary.

After a Boston nightclub fire, E. Lindemann worked with the disaster victims and their families. As a result of this experience he was able to formulate several general classes of normal grief. He was also able to describe some of the distorted reactions that one may see when grief is not satisfactorily resolved:[7]

1. Excessive activity with no sense of loss.

2. Development of symptoms similar to those of the deceased, often with related psychosomatic illness.

3. Alteration in relationships with friends and relatives. All social contacts may be shunned and the person become a recluse, or may need supervision because of giving away large sums of money.

4. Furious hostility against people associated with the death event, leading to letters of complaint and wishing to sue the hospital.

5. Behaviour resembling a schizophrenic pattern with lack of emotional expression, living in a daze, and acting in a 'wooden manner'.

6. Severe depression, with insomnia, guilt and bitter self-reproaches. Because the bereaved may feel the need to punish themselves for what has happened there is always an increased risk of suicide. 'I just want to die and be with him.'

A *clinical depression* following a death is frequently accompanied by other unresolved grief reactions such as guilt and self-blame. A young man, who had a tendency towards depressive illness, became depressed following the death of his baby daughter from an inherited disease. Before he and his wife were able to take up the appointment for genetic counselling he committed suicide. In a note he said that he felt genetically responsible for producing an abnormal child and that his wife would be better off without him. She could then marry a 'normal' man and have a normal family.

We earlier remarked that there is a need for 'society' to give permission to the bereaved to end formal mourning and where this does not happen the person can feel guilty and so unduly prolong mourning. Reassurance about one's responsibility for the death may be needed to allay guilt as in the case of a 'cot death' where remorse may lead to severe depression and the risk of suicide. The supportive role of groups such as the Foundation for the Study of Infant Deaths can be of vital importance in many such cases.

It is sometimes difficult for the lay person to distinguish between the sadness and 'depressed' periods of normal grief and a clinical depression. One of the main distinguishing features is that these episodes in normal grieving are transient and respond well to warmth and attention from other people. In clinical depression giving time and attention to the depressed person seem to have little effect and the person may seem to be just as low spirited and emotionally flat at the end of the visit as at the beginning. A referral to the general practitioner would then be indicated.

In some instances the person may withdraw into the past and preserve things as they were before the death. The classic example of this was Queen Victoria. She had a strong and dependent attachment to Prince Albert, to the extent that she became very upset if they were ever apart from one another during their married life. Such a dependent relationship, apart from any other factors, would have predisposed her to a severe reaction following his death. This has been well illustrated by the work of Lily Pincus,[8] a psychotherapist whose life's work as a marital therapist was given a new direction when she herself was widowed at the age of sixty-five years.

Lily Pincus maintains that marriages, and relationships generally, are based on two psychological principles: *projection and identification.*[9] People respond to bereavement in some measure according to which principle is stronger in their make-up. The couples who base their marital relationship on *projection* form complementary relationships in which the partners develop distinctly divided roles. In the event of a bereavement such couples seem to cope with the loss of their partner, because they are more secure in their autonomy. 'I feel as if something has been torn away from me' and therefore I am now separate and have an individual identity. After due mourning, such a death of a spouse may become a real time of growth and the survivor is seen to 'take on a new lease of life and to blossom'. If, however, too much of the self was projected on to the now lost partner, and if the projection was rigidly maintained, then the bereaved cannot separate sufficiently from the lost partner to truly bury him or her and pathological mourning may result.

The couples who built their marital relationship on *identification* and cannot bear to have differences, or to be apart from each other, find it especially hard to cope following a bereavement. This seems to be related to their having little sense of personal worth to help them face the world without their marriage partner and so they become increasingly helpless. 'It is as if something has died within me'; thus separation is not something that sets you free but entails loss of self as well. The person will therefore try to keep things as they were since that enables them to retain a sense of identity. This often shows itself through the setting up of a 'shrine' in the person's room so that it is ready for them to 'return to' at any time. A shrine can also be a way in which the bereaved can attempt to make perfect what in real life was far from perfect. So the mother who is bereaved of her very untidy teenage son may keep his bedroom ready for him to return to, but in a very tidy state and totally unrelated to how it looked when the son was alive. What is bizarre and atypical for one family may not be for another and such behaviour has to be assessed in context.[10] A widower, aged eighty years, who lovingly preserves his wife's dressing table as it always used to be is in a different category to the young mother who turns her dead child's bedroom into a shrine and allows no one to use it.

Identification can also manifest itself in the adoption of personality traits of the deceased and with the illness symptoms of the deceased. This may either show itself as hypochondriasis or with the conviction that one has the same disease that one's spouse died from. In such cases the pain experienced physically is real enough even though the cause may be psychological, and much reassurance may be needed from the family and the doctor, as well as encouragement to resume the social activities from which they withdrew into illness.

The minister of religion who is visiting the bereaved and identifies that grief is going wrong, or is unresolved, may be able to restimulate the grieving process by taking the person back to look at the events and feelings prior to the death and at the time of the death. If this does not lead to any movement forward for the bereaved person then it is necessary to consult with or refer the person for more specialist help. Apart from the general practitioner there are various other people and groups who may be able to help, according to what is available in the locality: health visitors, the community nursing service, social services who offer an emergency 'on call' service in most areas, and the various self-help and befriending groups such as Cruse, Samaritans, Citizens' Advice, counselling centres, Stillbirth Association, etc.[11]

If the minister is himself able to feel supported then he may be able to continue to support the bereaved person for longer and to continue his pastoral caring alongside, and in co-operation with, that offered by other professionals. This can be especially important when the referral has been to a psychiatrist, because of the fear of stigma which the bereaved may have. If the minister makes the referral and then drops out of the picture it may be interpreted by the bereaved that you are glad to have 'dumped' them on to someone else, or that now they are 'psychiatric' you won't want to know them. The *way* in which referral is made is as important as who the referral is made to.

The support of the minister in this aspect of his ministry raises the question of what is the role of the Christian congregation towards the bereaved in their community, and what sort of help and training might they need if they become actively involved in caring for the bereaved and the dying? What opportunities exist for the minister to develop insight and skills in this aspect of pastoral care and who can he turn to for help with *his* feelings arising out of this work? In the next chapter we look at 'the minister himself'.

Notes

1. S. Freud, 'Mourning and Melancholia', in *Complete Psychological Works of Sigmund Freud,* vol. xiv (1914-16), (Hogarth).
2. C. M. Parkes, *Bereavement* (Penguin, 1975), p. 142.
3. E. Lewis, 'Inhibition of Mourning by Pregnancy: Psychopathology and Management', *British Medical Journal,* 2, (1979), pp. 27-8.
4. See chapter 1, p. 4.
5. Lewis, op. cit., p. 27.
6. See bar chart on p. 57.

7. E. Lindemann, 'Symptomatology and Management of Acute Grief', *American Journal of Psychiatry,* 101 (1944), p. 141.

8. L. Pincus, *Death and the Family* (Faber, 1976).

9. *Projection* is the process by which we may interpret events and situations by reading our own experiences and feelings into them. In this way we may attribute our own feelings and motives to other people. *Identification* is the process by which we may unconsciously model our behaviour on that of someone to whom we are emotionally tied. Thus we may either extend our identity *into* someone else, borrow our identity *from* someone else, or fuse our identity *with* someone else. See Pincus (1976) p. 26ff for further discussion of these concepts.

10. A. Gardner and M. Pritchard, 'Mourning, Mummification and Living with the Dead', *British Journal of Psychiatry* 130 (1977).

11. See Appendix B for details of existing groups.

SEVEN

The Minister Himself

We have already looked at the customs and processes which may isolate the dying person and those close to him from the rest of the society of which they are part. Communities, however, usually give certain people unspoken permission to break the taboos and come near to the scene of the death. Doctors, nurses, funeral directors and ministers of religion seem to be the four categories of people who are today empowered to deal with the issues which surround death. In this chapter we will try to examine how the minister of religion may become more aware of his own needs in order to offer more effective help to others. John Hinton[1] says, 'The priest has for some people an essential part to play in preparing a person for death . . . There is much to be said for a doctor or someone who knows of the patient's fatal illness inquiring after his religious views so that "the minister can give continued help to the patient and his family so long as it is needed".' (A passing reference in the current *Dictionary of Medical Ethics*[2] mentions the special role of the minister of religion in caring for the dying.) Most clergy will know from experience that their duties are expected to involve visiting sick people at home or in hospital. The minister will bring with him, even before he speaks, a series of complicated expectations, both his own and those of the person he visits and much will depend on how aware he is of these expectations.

What Does the Minister Represent?

The minister visiting a sick person has a function which in some respects is different from that of others. The Ordination Service of the Church of England, paralleled in other ordinals and commissioning services, makes it quite clear that the minister is expected to visit a sick person, not on the basis of his sickness but of his humanity.[3] A person's illness may affect considerably the context of the visit and will involve the sensitivities of the minister in a particular way, but it does not of itself provide a reason for visiting. Ministers may often be tempted to ask a *diagnostic* sort of question, such as 'What is wrong with you?' Or they may be tempted to try to connect, often with the sick person's apparent connivance, the current crisis with something which has happened in the past, and try to answer the question, 'What have I done?'—which is a *moralistic* question. The question is, however, pastorally developed quite differently in the Book of Genesis[4] when God asks of the Adam or the Man, when they have lost sight of each other, '*Where* are you?' That is not, of course, offered as a crude pastoral technique but it remains a crucial question for the minister.

It has been the experience of the authors, as hospital chaplains, that in a crisis such as serious illness or bereavement the function which the minister of religion may fulfil at the first encounter may quite simply be that of a 'walking, talking visual-aid or ikon'. What he says may be much less important than what he is perceived to represent. One recent article[5] speaks of the clergy as 'the carriers of other people's longings' by which the author means that those who have consciously abandoned religious practice, even sometimes any sort of personal God, may have expectations of the clergy, almost as if the clergy have sometimes to represent for others beliefs which they may or may not consciously hold. The minister may find himself caught in a complicated situation in which his representative function demands that he speak with some sort of confidence, in which there is little space for his private feelings and beliefs.

It is one thing for a man to face up to the doubts in his own mind and the changes that are occurring around him. It is quite another thing to expect this man to confront the world as though he were perfectly confident in his views—especially if we are asking him to demonstrate his total and reassuring command in situations which tend to bring out feelings of anguish and impotence in most of us. The minister, in short, may be expected to say and do precisely the right thing in the death situation because he is really 'in the know'.[6]

So a considerable investment may be held even by those who have no formal religious belief in the representative role of the minister in terms of unchangingness and security. But his ability to behave, and sometimes to say things, which may sensitively challenge the established expectations may also be crucial. A hospital chaplain has told the authors of sitting by the bed of a small baby who was dying of a chronic disorder and not saying anything for a period of about ten minutes and then saying quietly, in response to a challenging question from the parents as to why this had been allowed to happen, 'I don't know'. He felt that he should have been able to say something rather more useful to the relatives but received a postcard from them two or three weeks after the child's death which said quite simply, 'Thank you for all the helpful things you said'. The resources of prayer and the sacraments, and sometimes the silent presence of the minister, often give structure and space to the expression of mixed feelings, such as hope and despair; joy and pain; faith and doubt.

The pastoral care which the minister gives is not, of course, something given by 'experts' to non-experts. The dying have much to teach the minister that he needs to learn for both his personal and his professional enrichment. He may find himself learning about himself and his ministry in a most remarkable way, for the dying person may have much to teach. A young priest was asked to say prayers with a woman in her eighties who was dying. He prayed with her and anointed her and was at that point very startlingly aware that his training in college had taken him no further than this point. He felt very inadequate and scared and began to repeat the prayers which he had said already, as he admitted later to himself to 'feel more comfortable' at the bedside of a dying person. It was his first encounter with death. His parishioner reached out and patted his hand. 'It's all right, you know,' she said. Her action changed the whole encounter, since they were caring for each other. Each felt able to offer something. Those involved in the Hospice Movement, which has developed the care of the dying so significantly, speak of how the dying patients in their care frequently helped and ministered to those who were officially caring for them.[7]

Two questions, we think, face the minister:
'How can I manage just to be there when other people may be doing practical tasks?' and
'How do I react personally, theologically and in my own spirituality to what is happening when someone with whom I am involved dies or when I am asked to take a funeral for someone whom I did not know?'

More than most others, the minister represents a tradition which has tried over the centuries to provide some framework for integrating individuals into a larger framework of experience which attempts to make sense of fundamental issues. No two people have exactly the same story of their life to tell. Early experiences, parents, siblings, important relationships and losses colour the way in which we perceive or reject ideas of God. The Judaeo-Christian tradition uses very personal language of fathers and sons, parents and children, brothers and sisters, and the minister brings the tradition with him by his presence.

Melvyn Thompson[8] explores three images of God commonly held, especially in the face of sickness and of death. The *first* is that God is indeed all-powerful and sends suffering as a way of punishing and keeping in order his Creation. God is understood as powerful but capricious. The *second* is that suffering is independent of God, who is loving and caring but impotent to do anything about it. The *third* is that God is involved with the forces of wholeness and integration in the face of illness and loss which has the power to disintegrate and destroy. The first two images are frequently those with which the minister may be endowed by those who encounter him, and indeed (particularly in the second) may represent how he sees himself. He may be seen as representing an all-powerful but fundamentally uncaring God, or being well meaning but powerless, capable of only offering palliative words and gestures. It is much harder for the behaviour of the minister to model[9] the third view.[10] Certainly it demands much more from him, and involves more personal theological and spiritual risk-taking, because it involves having to look at areas which are not clear and logical and where feelings may seem to be pulling in opposite directions. One minute a terminally ill person may be speaking with a lot of emotion about his death; at the next minute planning next year's holiday. The clergy may receive from those whom they visit very mixed messages of acceptance and rejection. One of the authors passed by the bed of a very sick woman who said to him, 'I don't know why you have come,' but at the same time patted the bed in an invitation to him to sit down. When he had sat down she delivered him a diatribe on the evils of organized religion but said at the end of the visit, 'You let me get angry with you, and stayed, and that helped'.

Sometimes the strong feelings which grief arouses can be expressed very forcibly to the minister and what he represents. On one occasion a minister who went to visit the parents of a child who had died in a road accident was met at the door by the mother rushing up and pummelling him. He did not leave the house but stayed and after a while the mother of the dead child put her arm on his shoulder and sobbed. What he seemed to do was to represent a God who did not exact retribution for her actions and strong feelings but who could stay with her physically and emotionally, not trying to change her or the situation but simply by being there.

Education for Death

So far we have spoken of the work which clergy may do at the time of death and bereavement and we shall return to this. But it may also be that the clergy may find their function with their parishioners or congregation will involve at least raising the issues of death and bereavement in sermons and seminars and in informal groups. These groups should also ideally include contributions from general practitioners, funeral directors, solicitors and other caring agencies. The role of the laity as representatives in visiting the dying and bereaved, especially post-bereavement visits, should be raised. In a society which finds endings and death difficult subjects to face, these issues may be raised with the clergy, often very informally, by those other than the formally religious and in settings other than the sick room or hospital. In hospitals the hospital chaplain may well have a special task of developing with hospital staff (medical students, student nurses and others) some of the issues involved in caring for the dying and bereaved. This is an essential piece of work, although paradoxically the view of the clergy as the 'death experts' may be reinforced just at a time when the traditions among Christians about Unction and Communion of the Sick may be changing precisely so that the church and the clergy are not viewed as only being concerned with the moment of actual death.

Making Contact

Obviously there will be a considerable diversity in the way a minister works with those whom he does not know well, and may only encounter at a time of crisis, and those who are in regular contact with him or the religious tradition he represents. With the former group of people the contacts he has may consist in the early stages of what might be called 'pre-counselling' and 'pre-evangelism'. It may take some time to find out exactly what are the feelings of the people concerned. How are they managing? What are their needs? For example, is their idea of resurrection the same as that of the minister? Language which may make considerable sense to the minister may not be experienced in the same way by others. Phrases like 'love of God', 'being saved' may have a significance associated with public worship which may not be the same in another setting. At the same time, Truax and Carkhuff[11] list among the attributes of a good helper the qualities of *genuineness* and *congruence,* suggesting that to be clearly at ease between the externals of what he represents and the internals of what he believes is something which provides a helper with his greatest asset. For the pastor who is ministering to the dying and bereaved this must involve facing the personal question, 'How do I feel about and face the possibility of my own death or of those close to me?' 'What are the points of contact inside myself between what I believe privately and express publicly?' 'Are the things I say, for example at funerals, the same things I learnt some time ago as an intellectual proposition?' 'How does my spirituality, what I believe and what I pray about, change or develop in the face of what I experience?'

More fundamentally, the minister may need to examine honestly his own need in the first place to enter a profession which is expected to cope with mortality and loss. What is sometimes called in psychological language *reaction formation* suggests that one may be drawn in one's choice of job or occupation to face precisely those areas in one's own life and background which have been difficult in order, as it were, to try and put those issues right at second hand through one's work. We are not talking about something which most of us 'know' consciously, but about something rather more hidden which will take some time and sensitivity to understand. Elizabeth Kubler-Ross tells of a student who denied any difficulty in facing dying people. When he was heavily pressed by his fellow students as to what he actually said it became clear that he did not go beyond the door of the room but just stood there and said 'God is love'!

Three attributes of the minister which, properly used and understood, are an essential part of the way he comes close to those facing death may become part of a system of *avoidance:*

1. His set-apartness through his ordination can lead to his being seen as having more access to the truth than others, and as the trustee of special qualities which are set aside for those who display special goodness.

2. His different style of dress, and his use of special language may, instead of being ways of making contact, become part of a *defensive* system which is basically protective of the minister, and which may make him less available.

3. His use of formal prayers and ritualized action may, instead of being a shared communication, protect him from a fuller relationship. Ritual is of its nature a general and public rather than specific and private way of communication.

His 'business', real or imagined, can lead to the impression that the dying or bereaved are receiving a special bonus in his hurried visits.

A number of studies made of those terminally ill patients who have clearly realized their diagnosis suggest that a far larger group than might be imagined realized that they were terminally ill.[12] They may not have admitted to themselves or talked to a staff member if in hospital, still less to their family and friends, but subsequently were able to pinpoint very accurately when the diagnosis was made. The minister may well find himself the person with whom the dying person, as one terminally ill man put it, 'tries on for size the possibility of his own death'. It is crucial for the minister to know what has been decided by those who are concerned with the care of the dying person. What decision has been made about informing that person of their prognosis? He will not usually be the person who is concerned with 'telling the patient'. He may be able to say when for example relatives insist that the person must not be told what is happening, 'Certainly your decision about telling him must be respected but do you think that he might be trying to tell *you* something?'

Language which speaks clearly and comfortingly to some people will not be heard in the same way by others. 'One person's most precious phrases are another person's cant.' Sometimes theological statements with which Christians might concur if used in the context of worship, like 'God is love', are often alienating if used in a different context. They may not then be seen as a statement about the nature of God and his Creation, but as attempting to justify the unjustifiable.[13] Religious activities and personnel are often seen as helping people to be 'good' and well adapted. Yet a minister who, by his presence and attitude, helps someone behave differently can sometimes let a person react to loss in a way that does justice to how they may feel, but at the same time may develop and change their view of God.[14]

A single woman in mid-life developed a fast-growing tumour. During her final hospital admission she remarked to the minister who visited her how strange it was that she had written a poem to God which began 'You whom I have loved and given everything and now You have betrayed me', and that she was also dreaming of children. She had been a long-standing communicant member of her church and had passed the age when having children was a possibility. Her minister, instead of replying to the unreasonableness of what she was saying and for which she was apologizing profusely since she felt it was 'wasting your time', listened for a while. He then said something about the place of anger and questioning as part of a Christian search for God and how often, especially when ill, one could look at unfulfilled possibilities in life and feel sad about them. She began to talk about what she called

122 _Letting Go_

her 'half-open doors'. She went back over her life and thought aloud about the events which had never quite come about exactly as she had predicted them. She seemed to present at this point in her illness two ways of coping. To those who did not know her well she presented what was usually called 'a brave face'. To the minister she talked about her 'lost possibilities' until she could finally say that she had now faced them and could let them go into God's hands. The minister and she prayed together with 'letting go' as a theme. It was crucial for her to recover some vision of a God who understood her other imperfect feelings and who did not try to correct false impressions as she faced the end of her life. The minister did not at first find it at all easy to understand what she was saying. He had to struggle too.

Ministers are sometimes asked outright by the dying person or his relatives, 'Is this all there is? Shall we meet again?' To answer the question with integrity according to the people and circumstances involved needs considerable discernment. When and who asks that question and how it is asked may affect whether the minister gives an answer from Scripture or from his own conviction or says something like, 'You must really miss him,' or, 'It's hard to let go people you love, isn't it?' The prospect of sharing in the resurrection of Jesus lies at the heart of the Christian gospel and it is that stand in the Christian tradition from which countless dying and bereaved people derive their hope.

But other factors may make it difficult for that message to be heard. Pastoral experience and surveys[15] suggest that the continuation of life after death is viewed in a number of ways, not all informed by Christian tradition, in the population as a whole. A considerable interest in reincarnation, of growth and development through many rebirths, or mysticism 'undogmatic by nature and experimental in character'[16] is in stark contrast to the Christian hope of resurrection, as developed in the tradition of both the Old and New Testaments.[17] A recent study[18] raises cogently the problem of preaching and speaking of the resurrection against such a confused background of belief and non-belief. The author tells the story of a family who wished the ashes of their father to be scattered on the local football pitch so that he could catch continuously the atmosphere of each Saturday's match.

This story illustrates poignantly, and reflects with some accuracy, a popular view of what happens at death. In spite of everything, things turn out all right and we survive, in some form, either to enjoy what death snatched away from us in this life or to experience a reversal of life's injustices, like Lazarus in the parable which Jesus told (Luke 16.19-31). Basic to this popular belief about life after death is the separation of soul and body and the immortality of the soul. Almost every *In Memoriam* column in the local paper provides evidence of this. 'Gentle Jesus up above, give our granny all our love.' Parents tell their children that granny has become an angel, even if that is hardly how they would have described her when she was alive. Our loved ones leave behind their bodies and go to a life where all is well, the inheritance of all sincere people who have kept the golden rule.

There is, of course, an important theological and pastoral distinction to be made. *Revivification* implies the person will come back to life just as they were. *Resurrection* is essentially a doctrine which encompasses the future and does not involve using the past as a basis for understanding the present or the future. 'A great deal of our difficulty when considering the future life is that we apply to it the logic of desire, instead of the logic of hope. We take it for granted that the form of our fulfilment in the future life will be modelled on what we desire as the people we are now. And this generally makes what we call heaven either ridiculous or frankly incredible or patently the projection of our own wishes onto the sky. But hope is the prospect of the radically new. It is the breaking in of what we had never dreamed of, a fulfilment beyond our desire to conceive.'[19]

Peter Selby's[20] exploration of the resurrection themes stresses the importance of the resurrection of Jesus as perceived corporately, to make sense of the future. The dialogue between Geoffrey Lampe and Donald McKinnon[21] sensitively discusses the resurrection of Jesus, whilst pointing out the danger of Christians appearing to offer a trivialized doctrine of what Lampe calls 'a corpse raised to life'. The pastoral implications of this debate are considerable.

The current confusion of attitudes which we have indicated makes the discussion even more germane and of considerable importance to the minister who cares for the dying and bereaved. A woman whose husband had suddenly died said to a minister colleague six weeks or so after his death, 'Something wonderful happened today. I forgot John.' She did not mean that she had ceased at that point to love him or miss him, but she had been terrified even to sleep lest her husband should disappear from her conscious memory. She found that she could forget him for moments when, for example, she was involved with her children, but she could also know that he was not completely lost to her. As she put it, 'his image can stay inside me', and her relief was immense. Her continuing love for her husband, and her sense of being close to him did not depend on her conscious effort.

The need to explore what is behind our understanding of the resurrection is an essential part of the minister's responsibility. But a balance needs to be maintained, and it is sometimes easy to give the impression that the physical body, or tangible needs, are of no interest to the minister.

> Because the clergyman is often viewed as on the side of the spirit with either a disregard of, or a turning away from, the physical side of life, it is important to articulate the goodness of the body and its important role in the whole economy of God. There is a need to be reminded that the creation story describes the creation of the world as 'good', and the creation of man from the dust of the earth as 'very good'. Man does not have a body or a soul. Rather, man is a body or he is a soul depending on the perspective at the moment from which he is viewed. Jesus's words, 'I thirst,' are a reminder of the physical side of life to both patient and pastor.[22]

Does Churchmanship Matter?

There is no easy answer to this question. Most ministers obviously need to work inside a tradition, since that usually provides them with their fixed points, some of their language and a system of familiar and significant words and actions. A minister's pastoral skill will come in his perception of how much the resources which he brings are of real or potential value to those with whom he may come into contact, or whether they may hinder his ability to meet people at a more than superficial level. How does he stand with integrity by some positions, but manage to be flexible about others? Are there other actions or words which can make the same point without distorting the meaning of what he may understand as vital. A seriously ill man from an evangelical Christian background in which free prayer was the norm was very appreciative of the ministry of the local vicar who came from a very different background because, as he said, 'he uses prayers from a book but they could be meant for me'.

In the chapter on rituals we discussed the place of rites of passage and the clergy are usually at the centre of, or much involved with, the rituals of dying and mourning. Being able to 'get it right' and to offer a liturgical form in terms of service at a crematorium or later at a memorial service may be more important than any other actions or words. A theological college principal said to his students, correctly we believe, 'Taking funerals may be one of the most important pastoral functions you will ever perform'.

The Personal Relations of the Minister

A minister will frequently develop relationships with people who are facing death which are very fulfilling, and he may feel at times that he is really doing the job for which he was ordained. But at other times the relationship may be more difficult to understand, especially if a person is expressing towards the minister or others strong emotions which are sometimes conflicting, of hate or love, or by apparently being very dependent and unable to make a decision without reference to him. It is not within the scope of this book to deal with some of the strong feelings which may take place in a pastoral relationship, except to remember that the representative role of the minister and his special access to people in crisis may lead to his being seen (or seeing himself) as endowed with particular qualities.

The psychological term 'transference' is a useful one since it means that the minister may be seen not just as himself.[23] In a situation of loss, his presence and sometimes his words can bring to the surface strong feelings which may belong, at an earlier stage of human growth and development, to another person, for example, father, mother or teacher. The minister in his turn may be surprised by the strength of his feeling about the people for whom he is caring. They too may acquire significance for him and come to represent people who have been an important part of his own past and background. We should stress that these feelings do not mean that the minister is doing a bad job from which he ought to withdraw rapidly. Properly understood they can provide a very useful and important way of caring more effectively.[24]

A minister's crucial role in bereavement or terminal illness may lead to either his over-involvement, where it becomes difficult to distinguish between his needs and those of others, or his withdrawal, perhaps saying that everybody is becoming too dependent upon him. Over-protectiveness is another danger and a good rule of caring is not to take away from anybody, however ill or however distraught, the ability to do things which, with support, they might hope to do for themselves. Alternatively a minister might feel that he only had something to offer to a dying or bereaved person if he visited bringing something tangible. One widowed man, when asked if his vicar had visited him, had replied with irritation, 'Yes, he came two or three times a week at first, but always with a little present. It was as if he found it hard to come by himself.'

Who Supports the Minister?

It is often easy to behave as if the giving of help is somehow a more worthwhile activity than the receiving of help so that the needs of a minister who is caring for the dying may be neglected by himself and by others. How the minister recognizes his own feelings and needs will deeply affect the way in which he copes. The Burial Service makes it clear that one of its functions is to remind those present, minister included, of their own mortality.

The question, 'What does the grief of others do to you?' is one to which we believe each minister has to be helped to find his own answer. As we have indicated, no two ministers will cope identically. Some may share their vulnerability with their families; others with their colleagues; others may bottle them up, perhaps only emerging to speak of crematorium fees as 'ash cash'! To manage well the pastoral care of the terminally ill and the bereaved is to face the question as to how much each person is prepared to allow painful and difficult experiences to reach him. When asked whether the constant experience of death ever 'got to' him, an experienced hospital chaplain remarked that if it did not move him just a little each time then he had no business doing his job.

Putting succinctly the idea of controlled involvement, T. S. Eliot wrote, 'Teach us to care and not to care'.[25] There are again lessons to be learnt here from the Hospice Movement[26] where the support of staff in groups and individually is seen as of prime importance. Some dioceses[27] have developed a network of support groups for clergy and pastoral workers which meet regularly and are one very valuable resource where those involved in pastoral care have been able to talk in confidence with a group of peers and raise some of their own needs for support. Individual needs are obviously very different, but we would stress that those clergy who obtain support and supervision are frequently those who manage best in situations like death which involve so closely the relationship between the personality, spirituality and practice of the minister. Clergy are also frequently able to make links between other people who may be involved in the care of the dying and the bereaved, bringing together others, doctors, nurses and social workers, possibly by means of a monthly bread and cheese lunch, frequently on church premises, arranged by the local clergy.

While we have concentrated in this chapter on ministers and their ways of working and particular needs, we would not want to suggest that the pastoral care is an exclusive function of ordained ministers. Much care to the dying and the bereaved is also given by lay people, and it would be presumptuous to imagine that ministers have a monopoly of pastoral skill or resources.

There may be occasions when the minister has become very attached to a particular parishioner who is dying and to the family. When that person dies he will also share in the sense of loss and experience the pain of letting go. Because he is the minister he may feel that he should be 'above' such feelings and, therefore, deny his own grief. If there are a series of such losses there can be an accumulation of unresolved grief with consequent need for personal support.

It can be tempting to take clergy and other caring people for granted and to assume that they do not have needs. Because of this they may suppress such needs and see them as inappropriate to their role. One valuable source of support for the clergyman should be the local Christian community and other members of the caring professions. However, we should not overlook the very valuable contribution that the patient can make in helping *us* to face the reality of death. If we couple this support with the words of St Paul, 'Not that we are sufficient of ourselves to claim anything as coming from us; our sufficiency is from God,'[28] we may learn to integrate death into our experience of living and thus find the 'courage to be'[29] with the dying and the bereaved.

Notes

1. J. Hinton, *Dying* (Penguin, 2nd edn 1972).
2. 'Interdisciplinary Relationships', *Dictionary of Medical Ethics* (Darton, Longman and Todd, 1981).
3. Church of England *Alternative Service Book,* p. 356.
4. Genesis 3.9.
5. The Bishop of Southwark's Advisory Committee for Pastoral Care and Counselling, Occasional Newsletter 1979.
6. R. J. Kastenbaum and R. Aisenberg, *The Psychology of Death* (Duckworth, 1974).
7. S. Stoddard, *The Hospice Movement* (Cape, 1979).
8. M. Thompson, *Cancer and the God of Love* (SCM, 1976).
9. By modelling we mean simply behaviour which may make what a person stands for more easily visible to others.
10. See John Hick, *Evil and the God of Love* (Macmillan, 1966) for an exposition of this third view.
11. C. B. Truax and R. R. Carkhuff, *Toward Effective Counselling and Psychotherapy* (Aldine Publishers, 1967).
12. Ian Ainsworth-Smith, 'At the Front Line of Dying', *Journal of Community Nursing* (October 1977).
13. C. S. Lewis, *A Grief Observed:* 'Talk to me about the comforts of religion and I shall suspect you don't understand.'
14. This becomes an opportunity for growth as described in chapter 1.
15. For example, the Opinion Research Centre study commissioned by the BBC into belief in life after death, *Sunday Telegraph* (13 October 1974).
16. I. Bunting, *Preaching at Funerals* (Grove Booklet No. 62, Bramcote, Notts., 1978), pp. 7-9.
17. 1 Corinthians 15.44: 'It is sown a physical body, it is raised a spiritual body.'
18. Bunting, op. cit.

19. H. A. Williams, *True Resurrection* (Mitchell Beazley, 1972).
20. P. Selby, *Look for the Living* (SCM, 1975).
21. G. W. H. Lampe and D. H. McKinnon, *The Resurrection* (Mowbray, 1966).
22. B. Schoenberg *et al.*, *Psychosocial Aspects of Terminal Care* (Columbia University Press, New York, 1972).
23. For further discussion of how the minister may cope with situations calling for specific counselling skills see H. Clinebell, *Basic Types of Pastoral Counselling* (Abingdon, New York, 1966); E. Kennedy, *On Becoming a Counsellor* (Gill and Macmillan, Dublin, 1977); M. Jacobs, *Still Small Voice* (SPCK, 1982).
24. A teenager's 'crush' on the curate would be a good example of this.
25. T. S. Eliot, 'Ash Wednesday—I', *Collected Poems 1909-1962* (Faber 1963).
26. S. Stoddard, op. cit.; see also an article with the rather sensational title 'Counteracting Burn-out for the Hospice Care-giver' by M. Friel and C. Tehan in *Cancer Nursing* (August 1980) which provides some excellent suggestions for supporting professional and voluntary helpers.
27. Notably in the Dioceses of Southwark, London, Rochester, Chichester and St Albans.
28. 2 Corinthians 3.5
29. P. Tillich *The Courage to Be* (Fontana, 1979). Alastair Campbell, *Rediscovering Pastoral Care* (Darton, Longman & Todd, 1981), pp. 26-64, gives a sensitive development of three biblical images, the shepherd's courage, the healer's wounds and the fool's wisdom. He suggests that the minister's ability to represent these images and to explore the meaning behind them is crucial both to his integrity and to his ability to help others.

APPENDIX A

Practicalities

The formalities and practicalities connected with death can seem daunting so we would like to examine a few 'nuts and bolts' issues, not with a view to answering all the questions, but indicating where might be the best source of further help.

The Hospice Movement

The modern hospice has become a skilled community which aims at improving the quality of life remaining for patients with long-term as well as mortal illnesses and sometimes for the frail and elderly. It accepts the patient with his family as the focus of its concern, involving them where possible as part of the caring team and supporting them in their bereavement.[1]

The word 'hospice' has a long history reminiscent at times of its medieval origins in feeding and housing those who were on a journey. 'Deep in our common mind and heart, as old as our civilization itself is the knowledge that hospitality is a duty owed to the weary traveller and to the sick.'[2]

The effect of hospices on care, not just of dying people, has been considerable, and has challenged widely held notions of success and failure in caring for the sick. Michael Wilson[3] and others have written how the curing of disease is frequently viewed as a more valuable activity than caring for those whose physical condition may not be curable but whose need for care is considerable. The *raison d'être* of the Hospice Movement is a better understanding of the nature of terminal pain and its relief. It is also attentive to the need for sensitive, imaginative and skilled personal care so that the dying person can live to the utmost of his ability and potential, physically, psychologically and spiritually. Hospices in the United

Kingdom have developed partly from the pioneer work of
institutions like St Joseph's Hospice, Hackney, and the Hostel
of God, Clapham (now called Trinity Hospice), but more
recently from the work and experience of St Christopher's
Hospice, Sydenham. An important development of the Hospice
Movement is Helen House in Oxford, planned to open in 1982
with accommodation for eight children with serious long-
term illnesses, some of whom will be terminally ill.[4]

Not all the patients who are cared for by hospices will be
treated on an in-patient basis all the time. An increasing
number of people are cared for in their homes by domiciliary
services. These are either staffed by the Hospice or organized
by the Macmillan Domiciliary Service. The latter is usually
supported wholly or partly by the National Society for Cancer
Relief and aims to provide home nursing and social support
where it seems best for the patient's care that they remain at
home. The Marie Curie Memorial Foundation provides in-
patient care for cancer patients at a number of residential
homes. Details of hospices and facilities for cancer patients
will be found in Appendix B.

Admission to a hospice is usually arranged through the
patient's own doctor in conjunction with the unit's medical
director, but each hospice will supply, upon request, details
of its admissions policy.

Making a Will

Details on the making of a will and managing the estate of a
person who has died are clearly set out in a Consumer
Association booklet.[5] The National Council for Voluntary
Organizations also produces a pamphlet dealing with death
which offers practical and concise advice, not only about
making a will but also other practical details.[6] They also
indicate the point at which the help of a solicitor may be
needed.[7] Information and advice on making a will or settling
an estate can be obtained from a local Citizens' Advice
Bureau. A guide to the help available in the form of death
grant and other benefits is provided in a Department of
Health and Social Security booklet.[8] A local Social Security
office will give more detailed information.

What to Do when Someone Dies

There are a number of procedures and formalities like registering the death and contacting a funeral director which should take place as soon as possible. An excellent guide to the practicalities is provided in the Consumers' Association booklet, *What to do when someone dies.*[9] A chart from that publication is reproduced here. It demonstrates the stages of registering a death and arranging a funeral. One point to bear in mind is that if a cremation is envisaged an extra medical certificate will be required from a medical practitioner who is not in partnership with the patient's own doctor. If death takes place at home this is something which the funeral director can arrange, and if in hospital a further certificate can be arranged on request.

Post-mortem Examination

The doctor who attended a person before death, either at home or in hospital, will usually issue a medical certificate showing the cause of death and a formal notice of death can be taken to the Registrar of Births and Deaths for registration. A post-mortem examination may be requested by the doctor if the nearest relatives agree. A typical form of consent which gives the usual reasons for the request is as follows:

> I do not object to a post-mortem examination being carried out on the body of . . . and I am not aware that he/she had expressed objection or that another relative objects.
>
> I understand that this examination is carried out:
>
> (a) to verify the cause of death and to study the effects of treatment, which may involve the retention of tissue for laboratory study.
> (b) to remove amounts of tissue for the treatment of other patients and for medical education and research.

The post-mortem examination usually takes place very shortly after death so it is rare for funeral arrangements to be affected.

What to Do when Someone Dies

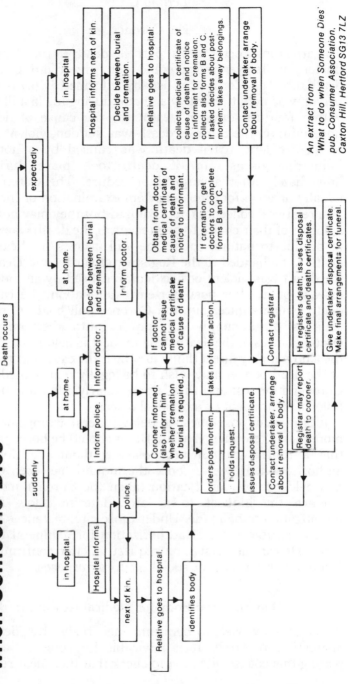

Death occurs

- **suddenly**
  - **in hospital** — Hospital informs next of kin. / police.
    - Relative goes to hospital. → identifies body
  - **at home.** — Inform police. / Inform doctor.
- **expectedly**
  - **at home.** — Decide between burial and cremation. → Inform doctor.
  - **in hospital** — Hospital informs next of kin. → Decide between burial and cremation. → Relative goes to hospital:

Coroner informed, (also inform him whether cremation or burial is required.)
- takes no further action.
- orders post mortem.
- holds inquest.
- issues disposal certificate
- Contact undertaker, arrange about removal of body.

If doctor cannot issue medical certificate of cause of death

Obtain from doctor medical certificate of cause of death and notice to informant.

If cremation, get doctors to complete forms B and C.

collects medical certificate of cause of death and notice to informant for cremation: collects also forms B and C. If asked decides about post-mortem: takes away belongings.

Contact undertaker, arrange about removal of body.

Contact registrar

He registers death, issues disposal certificate and death certificates.

Registrar may report death to coroner.

Give undertaker disposal certificate. Make final arrangements for funeral.

An extract from 'What to do when Someone Dies' pub. Consumer Association. Caxton Hill, Hertford SG13 7LZ

The Coroner

The attending doctor may report the death to the Coroner (a doctor or lawyer responsible for investigating certain deaths).[10] The Coroner is usually informed if (a) the dead person was not attended by a doctor during his last illness or within fourteen days of death; (b) the cause of death is uncertain; (c) the cause of death was sudden, violent or due to an accident; (d) if death was caused by a notifiable industrial disease; (e) if death took place during or immediately after a surgical procedure. The Coroner will usually arrange for a post-mortem examination of the body. The relatives' consent is not required but they may nominate a doctor of their choice to be present. If the death was shown to be due to natural causes he will issue a notification of death to be handed to the Registrar of Births and Deaths. If the death was violent or accidental, caused by an industrial disease or if, after post-mortem examination, the cause of death remains uncertain, the Coroner will hold an inquest. This is quite simply an inquiry into the cause and circumstances of the death. The inquest is held in public and the Coroner may direct that a jury hear the case. The relatives of the dead person may wish to be legally represented at the Coroner's inquest and this is particularly advisable if death follows an accident or industrial disease.

It is rare for an inquest to delay funeral arrangements by more than a few days, if at all. But it should be borne in mind that a funeral cannot take place without the Coroner's authorization. However, once the inquest has been opened and evidence of identification taken the Coroner may well adjourn the inquest to a later date to allow further investigation to be made. Under those circumstances he will usually issue a form of authorization for a funeral to take place. He can also issue, on request, a letter confirming the fact of death for legal or social security purposes.

Donation of a Body for Medical Research

A person may wish to bequeath their body after death for anatomical research. It is advisable for someone contemplating this course of action to check that their near relatives have no objection. Application (for England and Wales) should be made to: H. M. Inspector of Anatomy, Alexander Fleming House, London SE1 6BY — from whom a form of consent can be obtained which should be signed and witnessed and placed with other personal papers where it can be found after death. Alternatively the Professor of Anatomy at the local teaching hospital/medical school will be able to advise those considering donation.

Anatomical examination may extend over a period of up to two years. Once it is complete arrangements are usually made by the medical school concerned for a service of burial or cremation of the body conducted by a minister of the faith held by the deceased person in life. The next of kin can be informed of the date and time of the funeral if they wish.

As soon as possible after death the Inspector of Anatomy should be informed by the deceased person's executors or next of kin.

No guarantee can be given by the Inspector of Anatomy that a donation can be accepted. The place of death, and the cause of death are two factors which may affect his decision. A body from which organs have been removed for transplantation is not usually accepted for anatomical research.

I (full name, block capitals)

request that after my death:
*(a) any parts of my body be used for medical
   purposes; or
*(b) my *kidneys, *eyes, *heart, *liver, *pituitary
   gland, *pancreas be used for medical
   purposes.
*(delete if not applicable)
Signature   Date

In the event of my death, if possible contact:

Name (block capitals)   Telephone number

Donor card

Donation of Organs for Transplantation

The Department of Health and Social Security issued in December 1979[11] a Code of Practice which hoped to increase the supply of kidneys and other organs for transplantation. The relevant legislation[12] remains basically a system of 'opting in', usually by means of a card carried by the person which gives consent to the removal of specified tissue or organs (for example, kidneys, heart and eye corneas) after death. Opinion inside and outside the medical and nursing and legal professions is moving towards the establishment of an 'opting out' system under which organs could be removed in the absence of objection from a deceased person's next of kin. Legislation will probably be forthcoming in the near future which will reflect the change in emphasis. The Code of Practice clarifies the clinical definition of 'brain stem death' and discusses how a patient's relatives should best be approached for permission to remove organs for transplantation. Transplantation is most likely to be successful if organs are removed from a body as soon as possible after death has been certified.[13]

Notes

1. C. Saunders, 'Hospices', in *Dictionary of Medical Ethics* (Darton, Longman and Todd, 1981).
2. R. Lamerton, *Care of the Dying* (Penguin, 1980), p. 16.
3. M. Wilson, *Health is for People* (Darton, Longman and Todd, 1976).
4. Information on Helen House may be obtained from Mother Frances Dominica, All Saints Convent, 36 Leopold Street, Oxford OX4 1RU.
5. *Wills and Probate,* Consumer Association, Caxton Hill, Hertford SG13 7LZ.
6. W. M. Bowder, *Dealing with Death* (National Council for Voluntary Organisations, 26 Bedford Square, London WC1, 1980).
7. The names of solicitors who practise in a neighbourhood can be obtained from The Law Society (113 Chancery Lane, London WC2) or from a Citizens' Advice Bureau.
8. *What To Do after a Death* (D49, August 1979). Copies available from: Leaflets Unit, DHSS, P.O. Box 21, Stanmore, Middlesex HA7 1AY.
9. Consumer Association, Caxton Hill, Hertford SG13 7LZ.
10. In Scotland and Northern Ireland the procedures are different.
11. *The Removal of Cadaveric Organs for Transplantation — A Code of Practice* (HMSO, 1979).
12. Human Tissue Act 1961, 9 and 10 Eliz. 2, ch. 54.
13. R. Calne, 'Tissue Transplantation' in *Dictionary of Medical Ethics* (Darton, Longman and Todd, 1981).

APPENDIX B

Useful Addresses

Sue Ryder Foundation, Cavendish, Sudbury, Suffolk CO10 8AY
Cares for the physically and mentally ill, elderly and mentally handicapped people in residential homes.

Cruse, 126 Sheen Road, Richmond, Surrey TW9 1UR. (Tel. 081-940 4818/9047)
The national association for the widowed and their children.

The Compassionate Friends, The Administration Office, 6 Denmark Street, Bristol BS1 5DQ. (Tel. 0272 274 691)
A society of parents who have themselves experienced the loss of a child which seeks to help and support those whose children have died.

Stillbirth and Neonatal Death Society (SANDS), 28 Portland Place, London W1N 4DE. (Tel. 071-436 5881)
Supports those families whose children have been stillborn or died in infancy, and seeks to increase the awareness of those who come into contact with parents and relatives after the death of a baby.

Foundation for the Study of Infant Deaths (FSID), 5th Floor, 4 Grosvenor Place, London SW1X 8PS. (Tel. 071-235 0965)
Seeks to develop research into neonatal mortality.

Age Concern, Bernard Sunley House, 60 Pitcairn Road, Mitcham, Surrey. (Tel. 081-640 5431)
A major voluntary organization concerned with the needs of the elderly, including bereavement.

Support after Termination for Abnormality (SATFA), 29-30 Soho Square, London W1V 6JB. (Tel. 071-439 6124)

National Association of Bereavement Services, 68 Chalton Street, London NW1 1JR. (Tel. 071-388 2153)
Locally organized projects which offer practical and emotional support to the bereaved and also contact with trained and supervised volunteers.

Some Facilities for Cancer Patients

* Denotes a service initiated or supported wholly or partly by the National Society for Cancer Relief and bearing the name Macmillan

County	*Service Available*
Avon	
The Dorothy House Foundation, 164, Bloomfield Road, Bath BA2 2AT.	* In patient * Home care
St Peter's Hospice, St Agnes Avenue, Knowle, Bristol BS4 2DU.	In patient * Home care
Bedfordshire	
The Sue Ryder Home, St John's Road, Moggerhanger, Bedfordshire MK44 3RJ.	In patient
Berkshire	
Thames Valley Hospice Pine Lodge, Hatch Lane, Windsor SL4 3RW.	
Buckinghamshire	
Hospice of Our Lady and St John, Manor Farm, Willen, Milton Keynes MK15 9AB.	In patient * Home care
Cambridgeshire	
Arthur Rank House, Brookfields Hospital, 351 Mill Road, Cambridge CB1 3DF.	* In patient Home care
Cheshire	
Hospice of the Good Shepherd Gordon Lane, Backford, Chester CH2 4DG.	* In patient * Home care
Cornwall	
Macmillan Service, 3 St Clements Vean, Tregolls Road, Truro TR1 1RN.	* Home care

Mount Edgcumbe Hospice,   In patient
Porthpean Road, St Austell PL26 6AB.

Devon
Tidcombe Hall,   In patient
Marie Curie Memorial Foundation Home,
Tiverton EX16 4EJ.

St Luke's Hospice,   In patient
Stamford Road, Turnchapel,   * Home care
Plymstock, Plymouth PL9 9XA.

Dorset
Macmillan Unit,   * In patient
Christchurch Hospital, Christchurch BH23 2JX. * Home care

Essex
Macmillan Home Care Team,   * Home care
5 Cambridge Road,
Colchester CO3 3NS.

Gloucestershire
The Sue Ryder Home,   In patient
Leckhampton Court, Leckhampton,
Cheltenham GL51 5XX.

Hampshire
Countess Mountbatten House,   * In patient
Moorgreen Hospital, West End,   * Home care
Southampton SO3 3JB.

The Sue Ryder Home,   In patient
Bordean House, Langrish,   Home care
Petersfield GU32 1EP.

Hereford & Worcester
St Michael's Hospice,   * Home care
Bartestree, Hereford HR1 4HA.   * In patient

Hospice of the Marches,   Home care
Tarrington HR1 4HZ.

Kent
Wisdom Hospice,   In patient
St Williams Way, Rochester ME1 2NU.   Home care

Hospice at Home,   * Home care
Michael Tetley Hall, Sandhurst Road,
Tunbridge Wells TN2 3JS.

Lincolnshire
St Barnabas Hospice,   In patient
36 Nettleham Road, Lincoln LN2 1RE.   Home care

London

London Lighthouse, 111-117 Lancaster Road, Notting Hill, W11 1QT. (HIV, AIDS only)	In patient Home care
Trinity Hospice (Hostel of God), 29 North Side, Clapham Common SW4 0RN.	In patient * Home care
Continuing Care Unit, Royal Marsden Hospital, Fulham Road, SW3.	In patient
Macmillan Service, c/o St Joseph's Hospice, Mare Street, Hackney E8 4SA.	* In patient * Home care
St Christopher's Hospice, 51 Lawrie Park Road, Sydenham SE26 6DZ.	In patient Home care
St Thomas' Hospital, Palliative Care Team, Lambeth Palace Road, SE1.	In patient Home care
St John's Hospice, 60 Grove End Road, NW8 9NH.	In patient * Home care
Edenhall, Marie Curie Centre, 11 Lyndhurst Gardens, NW3 5NS.	In patient
Macmillan Continuing Care Team, St Giles' Hospital, St Giles' Road, SE5 7RN.	* Home care
Mildmay Mission Hospital, Hackney Road, E2 7NA. (AIDS only)	In patient Home care
Palliative Care Team, Royal Free Hospital, Hampstead NW3 2QG.	Home care

Manchester

St Ann's Hospice, Peel Lane, Little Hulton, Worsley, Manchester M28 6EL.	* In patient * Home care

Merseyside

St Joseph's Hospice Association, Ince Road, Thornton, Liverpool L23 4UE.	In patient
Marie Curie Centre, Speke Road, Woolton, Liverpool L25 8QA.	In patient

Middlesex
Michael Sobell House,   * In patient
Mount Vernon Hospital, Northwood HA6 2RN.   * Home care

Norfolk
Priscilla Bacon Lodge,   * In patient
Colman Hospital, Unthank Road,   * Home care
Norwich NR2 3TU.

Northamptonshire
Cynthia Spencer House,   * In patient
Manfield House, Northampton NN3 1AD.   * Home care

Nottinghamshire
Hayward House, Macmillan Unit,   * In patient
City Hospital, Hucknall Road,   * Home care
Nottingham NG5 1PB.

Oxfordshire
Sir Michael Sobell House,   * In patient
Churchill Hospital, Headington,   ᴬ Home care
Oxford OX3 7LJ.

Staffordshire
Douglas Macmillan Home,   * In patient
Barlaston Road, Blurton,   * Home care
Stoke-on-Trent ST3 3NZ.

Surrey
Sam Beare Continuing Care Service,   In patient
Weybridge Hospital, Weybridge KT13 8DY.   * Home care

Phyllis Tuckwell Memorial Hospice,   In patient
Trimmers, Waverly Lane, Farnham GU9 8BL.

Macmillan Continuing Care Team,   * Home care
Kingston Hospital, Kingston KT2 7QB.

Harestone,   In patient
Marie Curie Centre,   Home care
Harestone Drive, Caterham CR3 6YQ.

Sussex
West Sussex Macmillan Unit,   * In patient
King Edward VII Hospital, Midhurst GU29 0BL.   * Home care

Copper Cliff Hospice,   In patient
74 Redhill Drive, Brighton BN1 5FL.

St Barnabas Hospice,   In patient
Columbia Drive, Worthing BN13 2QP.   Home care

Macmillan Service,   * Home care
St Wilfrid's Hospice Project,   Home care
2 Millgap Road, Eastbourne BN21 2HJ.

Macmillan Service,   * Home care
13a Holmesdale Gardens, Hastings TN34 1LY.

Tarner Home,   In patient
Tilbury Place, Brighton BN2 2GY.

Tyne & Wear
St Oswald's Hospice,   In patient
Regent Avenue, Gosforth,   Home care
Newcastle-upon-Tyne NE3 1EE.

Conrad House, Marie Curie Centre,   In patient
Bentinck Terrace,   Home care
Newcastle-upon-Tyne NE4 6US.

West Midlands
St Mary's Hospice,   * In patient
Raddlebarn Road, Selly Park, Birmingham 29.   * Home care

Taylor Memorial Home,   In patient
76 Grange Road, Erdington,   Home care
Birmingham 24 0DF.

Warren Pearl House, Marie Curie Centre,   In patient
Warwick Road, Solihull, Birmingham BG1 3ER.   Home care

Compton Hospice,   * In patient
Compton Road West,   * Home care
Compton, Wolverhampton WV3 9DH.

Wiltshire
The Prospect Foundation,   * In patient
5 Church Place, Swindon SN1 5EH.   * Home care

Salisbury Macmillan Unit,   * In patient
Odstock Hospital,   * Home care
Salisbury General Infirmary, Salisbury SP2 8BJ.

Yorkshire
N. Yorkshire
St Leonard's Hospice,   In patient
185 Tadcaster Road, York YO2 2QL   Home care

S. Yorkshire
St Luke's Hospice,   In patient
Little Common Lane, Off Abbey Lane,   * Home care
Sheffield S11 9NE.

Macmillan Service,   * Home care
Royal Hallamshire Hospital,
Glossop Road, Sheffield S10 2JF.

W. Yorkshire

Wheatfields Hospice,
Grove Road, Leeds LS6 2AF.

In patient
* Home care

St Gemma's Hospice,
329 Harrogate Road, Moortown,
Leeds LS6 2AE.

In patient
* Home care

Overgate Hospice,
30 Hullen Edge Road, Elland HX5 0QX.

In patient
* Home care

The Sue Ryder Home,
Manorlands, nr. Keighley BD22 9HJ.

In patient
Home care

Ardenlea, Marie Curie Centre,
Queen's Drive, Ilkley LS29 9QR.

In patient

Wakefield Support Team,
c/o Clayton Hospital, Northgate,
Wakefield WF1 3JS.

Home care

Humberside

Dove House Hospice,
Chamberlain Road, Hull HU8 8DH.

* Home care

Scotland

Roxburghe House,
Tor-na-Dee Hospital, Milltimber,
Aberdeen AD1 0HR.

* In patient
Home care

Roxburghe House,
Royal Victoria Hospital, Jedburgh Road,
Dundee DD2 1UB.

* In patient

St Columba's Hospice,
Challenger Lodge, Boswell Road,
Edinburgh EH5 3RW.

In patient
* Home care

Fairmile, Marie Curie Centre,
Frogstone Road West, Edinburgh EH10 7DR.

In patient
Home care

Strathcarron Hospice,
Randolph Hill, Fankerton by Denny,
Stirlingshire FK6 5HJ.

In patient
* Home care

Hunters Hill,
Marie Curie Centre,
Belmont Road, Glasgow G21 3AY.

In patient
Home care

Wales

Amman Valley Hospital,
Glanamman, Ammanford, Dyfed SA18 2BQ.

* In patient

Brynseiont Hospital,
Caernarfon, Gwynedd LL55 2YO.

* In patient
* Home care

Monmouth General Hospital, Gwent NP5 3HP.	* In patient
Oakdale Hospital, Blackwood, Gwent NP2 0JH.	* In patient
South Pembrokeshire Hospital, Pembroke Dock, Dyfed.	* In patient
Treherbet Hospital, Rhondda, Mid Glamorgan.	* In patient
Royal Denbighshire Infirmary, Denbigh, Clwyd LL16 3ES.	* In patient
Bridgend Hospital, Y Bwthyn, Bridgend, Mid Glamorgan.	* Home care
Holme Tower, Marie Curie Centre, Bridgeman Road, Penarth, S. Glamorgan.	In patient Home care
Ty Olwen, Morriston Hospital, Morriston, Swansea SA6 6NL.	* In patient * Home care

Northern Ireland

Beaconfield, Marie Curie Centre, Kensington Road, Belfast BT5 6NF.	In patient
Northern Ireland Hospice, 74 Somerton Road, Belfast BT15 3LH.	In patient Home care

Eire

Our Lady's Hospice, (Irish Sisters of Charity), P.O. Box 222, Harolds Cross, Dublin 6.	In patient

Rehabilitation Services for Cancer Patients:

Colostomy
Colostomy Welfare Group,
38-39 Eccleston Square (2nd Floor), London SW1V 1PB.
Tel: (071) 828 5175

Laryngectomy
The National Association of Laryngectomy Clubs,
Fourth Floor, Michael Sobell House, 30 Dorset Square,
London NW1 6QL.
Tel: (071) 402 6007

Mastectomy
Mastectomy Association,
25 Brighton Road, South Croydon, Surrey CR2 6EA.
Tel: (081) 654 8643

APPENDIX C

Some Other Cultural Patterns

The rituals associated with death, more than many other rites
of passage, are closely identified with religion. The views
held by the group concerning an after-life and the future
mode of existence for the deceased will affect the ways in
which the dead are disposed of.

From the beginning of time man has been the only creature
known to bury his dead as an expression of his understanding
of the nature and destiny of man. Archaeological findings
indicate that when Neanderthal man died he was decently
interred with ornament shells and stone implements, which
he presumably might require beyond the grave. The
positioning of some corpses in a foetal position may reflect a
belief in rebirth. The binding of corpses, however, may well
indicate a fear of the dead and of their powers to harm,
especially if the burial rites had not been properly performed.
Linked to this we have the stigma which attaches to leaving
the dead unburied.

The stigma of leaving unburied dead relatives and friends,
so much explored in classical literature and elsewhere, can be
difficult to understand today when, if no one else can be
found who was close to the dead person, funerals are arranged
and paid for by local authorities or hospitals. Sophocles's
play *The Antigone* takes up vividly the theme of a sister who
takes terrible risks to bury her dead brothers. The Aeneid
tells of the unburied dead who cluster around Aeneas on his
journey to the underworld, unable to cross the Styx and find
rest. Similarly after a regiment of British infantry was
virtually annihilated in the Zulu War of 1879 at Isandhlwana
the two surviving companies who were quartered some
distance away insisted that the job of burying the dead was
theirs. Closeknit groups like regiments, medieval guilds and
the early Friendly Societies saw their duties to dead members

incorporating both the care of widows and children and the provision of an appropriate funeral.

The two themes which arise in the stories seem to relate to fundamental needs in the mourners, which the funeral rituals try to meet. Firstly there is the need for *reparation,* to have some ritual way of putting things right with and for the dead person, for ritual is a crucial way of 'acting the unsayable', especially where the circumstances of the death have been felt, because of accident, defeat or disaster, to be too terrible for words. Secondly, there is the need for *propitiation,* to put things right so that the dead person and/or the Gods cannot rebuke or even punish the living who have not done their proper duty by the dead.

We should emphasize that we do not believe that these themes represent beliefs that are consciously held by most people in the late-twentieth century but we are certain that the feelings which the minister may encounter frequently among newly bereaved people may only be understandable if he himself understands the fundamental and timeless issues which the old myths try to explore.

Perhaps the most obvious example of elaborate burial rituals is that found in ancient Egypt. Before 3100 B.C., in the Pre-Dynastic period, graves were shallow pits in the sand into which the contracted body was placed together with a few grave goods. The use of coffins later led to decomposition of the body, which in turn led the Egyptians to develop the art of mummification. Because the Egyptians believed that the physical body would be needed in the next life it was important to preserve it. The coffins frequently had painted scenes inside and out. These paintings and inscriptions usually included objects of use to the deceased in the next life, plus magical texts to safeguard the deceased on his journey through the underworld as well as to ensure his continued existence. The provisions for the next life sometimes extended to ensuring that certain deceased people might avoid *posthumous* conscription to assist with land reclamation on the Nile. Thus Deputies were provided in burials from the Middle Kingdom onwards in the form of *shabtis.* These people were mummified and given hoes, mattocks and baskets. It was believed that they could magically come back to life, because of the spell written on them, and dig the fields and irrigate the land in the name of their dead owners.[1]

The belief that the dead are going on a journey and therefore need provisions and a safe passage are reflected in other cultures. Burial excavations have shown that the Vikings buried their dead with objects used in life and that the ship was commonly associated with their burials to indicate the journey.

If the earthly body is of no further use after death then there is no need to go to elaborate lengths to preserve it. Hence, those religions and cultures which believe in reincarnation, or in the continuing existence of the spirit freed from the limitations of the body, are free to dispose of the body by fire. Buddhism, Hinduism and Sikhism all practise cremation and this is carried out with due respect for what the body has conveyed and expressed in life. Muslims and Jews for the most part practise burial although some liberal and reformed Jews may agree to cremation. In Christianity both burial and cremation are practised.

The rituals associated with death and dying do not replace the grief process but rather are offered as a helpful structure. The dying person, the deceased, the survivor and his social environment may find in the ritual an expressive act which will *aid the normal process of grief* and the status transition of both the bereaved and the deceased.[2]

An interesting example of this use of ritual is that seen in the patterns of mourning among the Yolngu of Australia, which illustrates the effects of urbanization on established cultural patterns.

The Yolngu[3] are Australian Aborigines who live in north-eastern Arnhem Land, Northern Territory. In this area many clans have moved out of the town and have 'gone home', and this has led to a cultural revival. However, the ancient rituals have had to be modified because of modern hygiene laws and urban influences.

The ritual commences before the death with people gathering to sing clan songs to comfort the dying and to keep his mind alert so that he may die in the right way. Frequently there is keening (or wailing).

When death occurs there is a dramatic change in emotional tenor of the group. The widow and other close kin throw themselves on the body, screaming and crying uncontrollably in their grief. Others are quiet. The senior men announce the death which is not openly acknowledged until the announcement. The women keen loudly, throw themselves on the ground and cut themselves on stones. The men may cry but usually express anger, which may lead to revenge attacks on other groups who are suspected of sorcery. The burial ceremony does not take place until everyone has arrived (a long time in Australia with large distances).

When the ceremonies have been arranged the body is collected from the hospital mortuary and taken, ceremonially, to the village. Car horns are sounded, there is singing and dancing. The body is placed in a shelter (usually in a large commercial refrigerator) which becomes the focal point for the community songs and dances. These songs act to effect *separation* for the deceased so that the spirit can travel to its right resting place. The lid of the coffin is decorated with sacred clan designs by the senior men, who alone see them.

Traditionally the body was placed on a platform for the birds to pick the bones clean prior to burial. Nowadays that is not allowed. The burial is accompanied by singing and dancing and a short ceremony conducted by a Christian minister. After he has gone some of the men return to 'switch' with leaves of burning branches to chase away the spirit. Those concerned with the burial are unclean and require ritual washing. Several months or even years later further ceremonies may be held to cleanse the house of the deceased for habitation. Traditionally the bones would be recovered, cleaned, placed in a bark coffin, which was decorated and placed upright (as a totem) exposed to the elements until eventually it decayed away. This is no longer widely practised in Arnhem Land, but sufficient of the ritual is retained in modified form to facilitate the grieving of the relative.

Mourning for the Yolngu is structured, guided and limited and it is expected to be publicly expressed. The reality of the death is clearly demonstrated to the bereaved and expression of emotional reaction encouraged, with visible social support. In the conclusion of her article on the Yolngu, Janice Reid writes:

'In northeastern Arnhem Land the mortuary ceremonies not only affirm in dramatic form the relations and beliefs of the living, but enable the bereaved to mourn in a culturally structured and contained context, to resolve grief and to resume social roles. In short, mortuary ceremonies afford the bereaved "a time to live" and "a time to grieve".'

Whilst the traditions of the Yolngu may not be applicable to our own culture, the way in which they employ ritual and have adapted not dispensed with it in the face of urbanization, has much to say to us in our management of grief.

Notes

1. British Museum Guide (1976), p. 35 ff.
2. For an excellent historical perspective of customs, literature and rituals from the Middle Ages to the present day see P. Ariès, *Western Attitudes to Death* (M. Boyars, 1976) and *The Hour of our Death* (Allen Lane, 1981).
3. These notes on the Yolngu are based on a very graphic and detailed account by Janice Reid, 'A Time to Live, A Time to Grieve', *Culture, Medicine and Psychiatry.* 3 (1979), pp. 319-46.

Select Bibliography

Anthony, S., *The Discovery of Death in Childhood and After.* Harmondsworth, Penguin, 1973. (Readable and important study of how children develop a concept of death.)

Bowlby, J., *Attachment and Loss vol. III: Loss.* Harmondsworth, Penguin, 1981. (A very important and basic text.)

Burton, L., *Care of the Child Facing Death.* London, Routledge & Kegan Paul, 1974.

Gordon, R., *Dying and Creating — A Search for Meaning.* London, Society of Analytical Psychology, 1978.

Hill, S., *In the Springtime of the Year.* London, Hamish Hamilton and Penguin, 1974. (A novel providing valuable insight into the world of the bereaved.)

Hinton, J., *Dying.* Harmondsworth, Penguin, 1972 (2nd edn). (Important and careful study.)

Kubler-Ross, E., *On Death and Dying.* London, Tavistock, 1970. (Essential reading.)

Kubler-Ross, E., *Death, The Final Stage of Growth.* London, Prentice Hall, 1975.

Lamerton, R., *Care of the Dying.* Harmondsworth, Penguin, 1980.

Lewis, C. S., *A Grief Observed.* London, Faber, 1973. (A classic.)

Parkes, C. M., *Bereavement.* Harmondsworth, Penguin, 1975. (Essential reading.)

Pincus, L., *Death and the Family.* London, Faber, 1976.

Prickett, J. (ed.), *Death.* Living Faiths series, London, Lutterworth, 1980. (Death in other cultures plus valuable resources for inter-faith ministry.)

Simpson, M. A., *Dying, Death and Grief.* New York, Plenum, 1979. (A critically annotated bibliography.)

Smith, JoAnn K., *Free Fall.* London, SPCK, 1977. (A dying person's personal account.)

Solzhenitsyn, A., *Cancer Ward.* London, Bodley Head, 1968.

Speck, P. W., *Loss and Grief in Medicine.* London, Bailliere Tindall, 1978.

Spiegel, Y., *The Grief Process,* London, SCM, 1978. (Repays careful reading.)

Tolstoy, L., *The Death of Ivan Illych.* New York, New American Library, 1969.

Zorza, R. and V., *A Way to Die.* London, André Deutsch, 1980. (A very moving account of the life and death of a 25-year-old woman by her parents.)

Articles in Periodicals

Stillbirth and cot death

Harman, W. V., 'Death of my baby' (*BMJ*, 282, 1981) pp. 35-7.
Lewis, E., 'The management of stillbirth—coping with unreality' (*Lancet*, ii, 1976) p. 620.
Limerick & Downham, 'Support for families bereaved by cot death' (*BMJ* 1 (6126), 1978) pp. 1527-9.
Speck, P., 'Easing the pain and grief of stillbirth' (*Nursing Mirror*, 1 June 1978) pp. 38-41.
Weinstein, S. E., 'Sudden infant death syndrome' (*Am.J.Psychiatry*, 135(7), 1978) pp. 831-4.

The dying child

Black, D., 'The bereaved child' (*J. Child Psychol. Psychiatry*, 19(3), 1978) pp. 287-92.
Chapman, J. A. & Goodall, J., 'Helping a child to live whilst dying' (*Lancet*, 1(8171), 1980) pp. 735-6.
Currie, S., Morrell, C., Mitchell, M., 'Death, the child and his family—a stay at Burrswood' (*Nursing Times*, 76(25), 1980) pp. 4-7.
Peck, B., 'Effects of childhood cancer on long-term survivors and their families' (*BMJ*, 1(6174), 1979) pp. 1327-9.

Hospice and home

Hinton, J., 'Comparison of places and policies for terminal care' (*Lancet*, 1(8106), 1979) pp. 29-32.
Lamerton, R. C., 'Cancer patients dying at home. The last 24 hours' (*Practitioner*, 223(1338), 1979) pp. 813-17.
Luxton, R. W., 'The modern hospice and its challenge to medicine' (*BMJ*, 2(6190), 1979) pp. 583-4.
Parkes, C. M., 'Terminal care: evaluation of in-patient service at St Christopher's Hospice' (*Postgrad.Med.J.*, 55(646), 1979) pp. 517-27.

Miscellaneous

Greenblatt, M., 'The grieving spouse' (*Am.J.Psychiatry*, 135(1), 1978) pp. 43-7.
Lieberman, S., 'Nineteen cases of morbid grief' (*Brit.J.Psychiatry*, 132, 1978) pp. 156-63.
Reid, W. S., Gilmore, J., Andrews, G., Caird, F., 'A study of religious attitudes of the elderly' (*Age and Ageing*, 7, 1978) pp. 40-5.
Pinney et al., 'The dark side of nursing' (*Nursing Mirror*, 148(14), 1979) pp. 14-20.
Chapman, C. et al., 'Care of the terminal patient' (*Nursing Times*, 75, 1979). Ten articles between pages 487 and 845.
Grainger, R., 'The funeral as a work of art' (*New Blackfriars*, 61 (719), 1980) pp. 181-4.

This short bibliography is only a small part of the vast number of books and articles currently available. It is our hope that readers will find the references in the above works a means of further extending their study.

Index

Abnormality 46-7
Absolution 69
Accidental death 2
Adolescence, death in 48-51
After-life 26, 145
Aims, pastoral 65-6
Anger 7-8, 17-18, 83
Anniversary of death 97
Anointing 19, 29, 68, 70,
  71-2
Anxiety 15, 84
Ashes, interment of 98
Awareness 6, 23; cones of
  32 (diagram)

Baby, death of 44-7;
  funeral of 44-5;
  abnormal 46-7
Baptism of the dying 68-9
Bereavement behaviour,
  normal patterns of 13
  (diagram), 30-1
Bible reading with the dying
  66-8, 73
Body, loss of one's 25-6;
  change of image 41; of
  dead baby 44; viewing of
  76-7
Buddhism 26, 147

Certificate of death 76
Change, and loss 37-43; in
  physical appearance 41;
  of body image 41
Chaplain of hospital, role of
  18-19, 24, 66, 68-74, 76,
  82, 92

Child, death of 48-52
Children, and funerals
  101-2; and attitudes to
  death 51-2, 101
Churchmanship 124-5
Commendatory prayer
  73-4, 80
Communication 29, 67
Concept of death 51-2
Cones of awareness 32
  (diagram)
Confession 69-70
Confirmation of the dying
  69
Contract funeral 91
Coroner 76, 134
Cot death 45-6, 110, 137
Counselling centres 112
Cremation 147
Cruse 12, 112, 137
Cultural patterns and
  customs 26, ch.5, 145-9

Death, of a baby 44-6; in
  childhood 48-51; in
  adolescence 48-51; of a
  pet 39-40; sudden 52-
  4; in old age 54-5; at the
  time of 74-6, 132-3
Death-bed marriage 72-3
Denial of death 5-6, 52,
  107-8
Depression 10-11, 28-9,
  109-10
Development and growth
  35-43
Dignity, loss of 27-8

Disbelief and shock 5-6, 20-3
Divorce and grief 84, 108
Donation, of body for research 78, 92, 134-5; of organs for transplantation 75, 135, 136

Education for death 118-19
Emotions 25-6; response to emotions of dying 31

Family, loss of 25-6
Fear 24-7, 145
Forgiveness, sacrament of 69-70
Friends, loss of 25-6
Funeral, place in grief process 12-14, 79; ritual of the 78-95; of baby 44-5, 76; children attending 101-2; non-Christian 91; where there is no body 92-3

Grave 98
Grief 1-14, 35, 96; resolution of 11-14, 28-33; work 55-9; place of ritual in grief process 62-74, 103, 147; delayed 106; public 53; private 54; classification of 'normal' grief 109
Growth and development 35-43
Guidance in pastoral relationship 65
Guilt 8-10, 23, 84, 106

Handicapped child 46
Headstone 98
Hindu religion 91, 147
Holy Communion 19, 70-1, 89, 101
Hope 24
Hospice Movement 27, 116, 127, 130-1; for children 51, 131

Hospital chaplain, role of 18-19, 24, 66, 68-74, 76, 82, 92

Identification, relationship based on 111, 113
Images of God 117
Incorporation 60, 70, 79, 101
Independence, loss of 27
Inquest 134
Interment of ashes 98

Jewish religion 75, 77, 94-5, 147

Laying on of hands 72
Laying out 74-5
Loneliness, fear of 26-7
Loss 25-8, 36-43

Marriage, death-bed 72-3
Memorials 98
Minister, relationship with 29, 64, 125-6; support for 126-8; the minister himself ch. 7
Miscarriage 46
Muslim religion 75, 77, 147
Myths surrounding death and burial 145-9

Needs, response to needs of dying 31, 53

Old age, death in 54-5

Pain 26-7, 130
Pastoral aims 65-6
Penance, sacrament of 70
Pet, death of 39-40
Physical appearance, changes in 41
Post-mortem 77-8, 132
Prayer, for serenity 28; of commendation 30, 73-4, 80; with the dying 66-8; with the family 82; for the dead 99-100

Pregnancy and grief   107
Problems of grief   ch. 6
Projection, relationship
    based on   110-11, 113
Prolongation of grief   108-9
Propitiation   146
Purgatory, doctrine of   99

Reconciliation in the pastoral
    relationship   37, 65, 69
Registration of death   76,
    132
Regression   37
Reincarnation   26
Reincorporation   70, 93
Relationship with minister
    29, 64, 125-6
Reparation   146
Resolution of grief   11-14,
    28-33
Response, to emotions of
    dying   31; to needs of
    dying   31, 53
Rites of passage   ch. 5, 125
Ritual, prior to death   62-
    74, 147; at the time of
    death   74-8, 147; follow-
    ing death   78-102, 148

Sacrament, of baptism   68-
    9; of forgiveness   69-70;
    of Holy Communion   70-
    1; of anointing or unction
    71-2; of marriage (death-
    bed)   72-3; of the sick
    71
Sadness   10, 29

Sedation   10
Separation   34-43, 61, 70,
    79-83, 148
Sermon in the funeral service
    89-92
Service, thanksgiving for
    birth of child   47; for
    suicide   48; funeral   78-
    95; memorial   125
Shock and disbelief   5-6,
    20-3
Shrines   4, 7, 111
Sikh religion   91, 147
Stillbirth   6, 7, 44-5, 76
Sudden death   52-4
Suffering, fear of   26-7
Suicide   47-8, 109
Support   31; for minister
    126-8
Sustaining in the pastoral
    relationship   37, 65

Transference   125-6
Transition   60, 70, 79,
    84-93
Transplantation of organs
    75, 136

Unction   *see* Anointing

Viaticum   70-1
Viewing the body   76-7
Visits by clergy, pre-funeral
    81-3; post-funeral   95-8

Will, making a   131